EELS
A Natural and Unnatural History

EELS

A Natural and Unnatural History

CHRISTOPHER MORIARTY

UNIVERSE BOOKS
New York

Published in the United States of America in 1978
by Universe Books
381 Park Avenue South, New York, N.Y. 10016

© Christopher Moriarty 1978

Library of Congress Catalog Card Number: 77–24784
ISBN 0–87663–293–2

Printed in Great Britain

CONTENTS

PREFACE

In 1959, when I entered the Irish fishery service, the director of the laboratory said 'You do eels'. I have been doing them ever since and will be happy to continue. The study of any animal can easily become an obsession. A single species or even an individual is such a complex being that no research worker can hope to discover much about it in a lifetime, since every problem solved poses a hundred more. Hydra merely produced two heads for every one that Herakles severed. He was a lucky man to be confronted with so simple a task.

So, sixteen years later, I know very little about eels. But these fish are so interesting and so much a part of the lives of fishermen, zoologists and people who simply love country life that it seemed worthwhile to set down some of the facts and speculate on a few of the many mysteries.

1

INTRODUCTION

On dark autumn nights, when floods have swollen the rivers, eels swim silently downstream, heading for the sea. Millions are caught by fishermen whose forebears have known the eels' movements for thousands of years. Great numbers escape the nets and disappear for ever in the ocean.

In spring, as soon as the water of the same rivers warms up a little, even greater numbers of elvers, little eels the size and shape of darning needles, appear at the beginning of a journey upstream. Between these appearances the eels feed and grow in fresh water but always unobtrusively, seldom noticed by anyone but fishermen and a handful of biologists. In spite of their retiring habits eels are well known fish. The very name has passed into everyday speech while their ability to wriggle out of difficult situations is proverbial.

Informed interest in eels dates at least to the fourth century BC when Aristotle recorded many of the facts and unleashed speculation on the mysteries of their lives. The breeding place of the freshwater eels of Europe and America was unknown until Johannes Schmidt's voyages in the present century, and the exact spawning sites of Japanese, Australasian and Indian Ocean eels are still unknown. At the time of writing no sexually mature freshwater eels have been seen in the wild. On this basis one scientist has inferred that eels never breed at all. But fishermen are not in the least surprised that the elusive adults have not been caught in the depths of the ocean.

Writings on eels are abundant. A bibliography of freshwater eels alone, compiled by Professor Meyer-Waarden and Dr E.

Introduction

Aker in Hamburg in 1966 contains 3,400 titles. Books on eels on the other hand are very few. Only one on eel biology in English is in print and a German work was published in 1973. My background is that of a fishery biologist who has been studying the food, growth rate and population of Irish freshwater eels, work which led naturally to the need to become a practical fisherman. The fine flavour of my specimens combined with a deep dislike of throwing away food made me investigate many ways of cooking eels. My experiences in these fields provides the basis of much of this book.

Many volumes could be written on the biology of the European eel alone. But biology is only one facet of an edible animal and the methods of capture, transport, rearing and preparation are equally interesting. My approach therefore has been to consider first such subjects as the feeding habits, behaviour and general ecology of the eel. These are the basis of eel fishing and eel culture which lead ultimately to cooking.

While the freshwater eels are the most fully investigated and the most important as food fish, they are a minor group in terms of variation. The marine eels run to several hundred species. Most of them live in the shallows of tropical and sub-tropical seas but a number have established themselves as important members of the deep-sea fauna. Besides their general interest as fish, the life cycles of the marine eels have a bearing on those of the freshwater species.

EELS AS ANIMALS

The eel is undoubtedly a fish. The long and sinuous body gives the impression of a snake or outsize worm. But this is one of the cases where animals of widely differing kinds, true worms, reptiles and fishes, have independently developed a body form suitable for burrowing or gliding through dense cover.

Freshwater eels can be recognised as fish at once by their fins. A dorsal fin runs down the back as a long fringe, merges with the tail and continues forwards underneath to the anus as

10

an anal fin. The border of head and body is marked by the position of a pair of pectoral fins, corresponding to the forelimbs of higher animals. The second paired fins, present in most other fishes, are not found in modern eels although they may be seen in fossil species. Fins are even more reduced in many of the marine eels. The morays lack pectorals and some of the snake eels have no fins whatever.

The internal anatomy distinguishes even the finless eels from reptiles. In particular, they breathe like all fish by means of gills. Water is drawn in through the open mouth, passes over the gills and out through the gill openings which are small holes a little way in front of and below the pectoral fins. Oxygen, dissolved in the water, is extracted by the gills. Eels therefore cannot live indefinitely out of the water. They can, however, survive on land longer than most other fish. Indeed they are so vigorous when caught that I usually place my captives at once in anaesthetised water in the bottom of a large dustbin. Otherwise they have a disheartening way of leaping out of a small boat or hiding beneath the floorboards. Freshwater eels on migration will leave the water if they meet a barrier and can make long journeys through wet grass. Little eels wriggle through damp moss in preference to trying to swim up a waterfall and there are records of eels crawling out on the land to forage.

Just as they can survive for some time on land, eels are exceptionally well able to resist water pollution. I was once advised not to search for eels in the river Barrow because nothing had survived a fish kill a few weeks previously : I discovered that the eel population had remained at full strength. When de-oxygenated water passes down a river the eels are able to retire to their burrows and rest, using very little oxygen, while other fish have to maintain a high rate of respiration. Even eels cannot survive these conditions indefinitely but they are exceptionally tolerant.

The ability to travel on land is associated with the burrowing habits. Eels produce large quantities of mucus which serves to lubricate them as they burrow. This slime has considerable water-retaining power so that on land the eels can keep their body surface moist. A certain amount of respiration can take place through the skin and survival for forty-eight hours out of the water is possible, always provided a little moisture is available. Eels left out of the water in a dry place on a sunny day expire relatively quickly.

EELS AS FISH – THE LIFE CYCLE

The life cycle of eels even today has an air of mystery about it. The earliest written records date to Aristotle, who stated quite simply that the eel is neither male nor female and can engender nothing. He believed that eels arose by spontaneous generation from mud or slime, a belief which continued to be held for centuries and dies hard in country places. It was a reasonable idea : while the developing eggs of the majority of common fishes can be seen clearly if the female is opened at the right season, the ovary of the eel is inconspicuous – almost invisible in young specimens and forming no more than a whitish, frilled ribbon in more mature ones.

Even if the eggs had been recognised, the form of the very young eel would have caused problems. Although the arrival of elvers or small eels from the sea had been known for centuries, the fact that all eels, freshwater and marine, have a long larval life was not understood until the nineteenth century. 'Larva' is the term used to describe the free-living young of an animal when it has a distinctly different form from the adult. The first eel larva on record was caught in 1763 by one William Morris in the Irish Sea near Holyhead, north Wales. It was transparent, with a ribbon-like body and a tiny head. Later it was discovered first that this creature was a larval form, not an adult fish, and next that it was an eel. Finally, in 1886, M. J. Delage announced that he had observed the metamorphosis of one of this species to a baby conger eel. In 1896, S. Calandruccio and B. Grassi at Messina recorded the metamorphosis of the freshwater eel from a marine larva. They quite reasonably believed that the eels bred in very deep water in the Mediterranean. Had they spawned in the shallows the ripe adults would surely have been caught from time to time.

The weak point in the theory of a Mediterranean spawning ground was that no small larvae were found there. The approximate position of what has turned out to be the sole breeding ground of the European eel was discovered by the Danish oceanographer and fishery biologist Johannes Schmidt. Applying a technique he had developed when searching for the spawning places of the cod, Schmidt drew a sort of contour map of the lengths of the larvae found in plankton hauls across the Atlantic. The smallest specimens were found in the Sargasso Sea and the same was true of the larvae of the American freshwater eel.

Schmidt concluded that European eel larvae take about two and a half years to cross the ocean from the Sargasso Sea, making them amongst the longest-living larvae of any fish. Such immense journeys are not too uncommon amongst eels. Unfortunately none of the breeding places of the other freshwater species are known for certain but migrations of one, two or three thousand miles are probably normal. The European conger is another distant traveller. An Atlantic marine eel which breeds near the Cape Verde Islands travels to the Gulf of Mexico, taking the opposite route across the ocean.

These long-journeying eels spawn once in their lifetime and die soon afterwards and no adult has been known to make a return journey. The majority of known species of eels are coastal fish but they all appear to migrate offshore to deep water to breed. Knowledge of spawning habits is extremely limited. Where the breeding places are known it is usually as a result of deduction from the presence of small larvae or sometimes eggs rather than by any direct observation. Some worm eels in the Philippines breed close to Manila Bay in summer, and both adult and larval thread eels are found together in deep ocean water off the Bermudas. The essential need for eel breeding seems to be deep, warm water : as so many live most of their lives in the shallows the habit of migration is the general rule.

Introduction

The freshwater eels are considered the most primitive family in the group. A 'primitive' anatomical structure does not necessarily mean that the species concerned are in any way unfitted for life. Amongst the mammals the plan of the human body is one of the more primitive. This merely indicates that the structures developed at an early stage in the evolution of the group were so perfectly fitted for life in certain conditions that relatively few alterations were needed. The earliest fossil eels can be traced to the Cretaceous era and several genera which exist today have been found in Eocene and Miocene strata.

Freshwater eels are, as eels go, of moderate length relative to their girth. Their mouths are small and the teeth are fine, rather rasp-like, adapted for gripping small animals which are then swallowed whole. The eels of temperate rivers are all uniformly coloured : shades of yellowish or greenish brown on the upper side. A number of the tropical species have mottled colouring, showing shades of green or yellow with brown. The National Museum in Dublin has one freak specimen of European eel showing green and yellow mottled colouring.

Female eels grow very much bigger than males. Some tropical species reach a length of 2m but the Atlantic and Japanese eels are smaller, of the order of 1m and often less. Male European eels rarely grow longer than 45cm.

Small teeth and moderately thin bodies with well developed fins are the commonest characteristics. The small teeth are typical of eels which feed chiefly on invertebrates, but a number of genera are primarily fish-eaters and have developed exceedingly powerful jaws with savage-looking fangs. The conger-pikes, found in tropical seas around the world, have large mouths armed with formidable canine teeth not only on the edges of the mouth but also on the palate. The congers also have strong, sharp teeth. Still with the general shape of eels, the morays show the beginning of loss of the fins : they retain dorsal and anals but the paired pectorals are absent. Most of the morays are

14

large-mouthed fish-eaters with a reputation for savagery, but one genus has small molar-like teeth apparently for crushing shellfish. Reduction of the fins reaches its extreme in some of the snake eels which are completely finless. The biggest eel of all is the giant moray of the Indo-Pacific coasts which reaches a length of 3m.

Deep-sea eels in general are well endowed with fins. Some congers live in the depths as do other typical eels but some of the commonest kinds have extraordinarily developed bodies. Fantastic elongation of the jaws is found in many species, among them the thread eels and snipe eels. These jaws are long and almost wire-like but provided with rows upon rows of fine, backward-pointing teeth. In spite of their weak appearance these jaws can take a firm hold of relatively large shrimps and manoeuvre them into the narrow throat of the eel. The bodies of the thread eels are immensely long, even by eel standards,

Illus 1 A broad-headed yellow eel, *Anguilla anguilla*. This is an immature female, length 61cm, weight 444g, age 23 – a slow growing specimen

and contain several hundred vertebrae in contrast with the normal hundred or so. At the other extreme, amongst the deep-sea eels is a little species with a truncated body and exceptionally tall fins. Finally there are the extraordinary deep-sea slime eels : lamprey-like creatures with small mouths which live parasitically on other fishes. Some details of the varieties of eels are given in Chapter 9.

An unusual feature of the head of many eels is the presence of a pair of short tubes on either side of the upper lip (Illus 1). These are the front nostrils, used in sniffing for food. Although freshwater eels have well-developed eyes which become greatly enlarged at the time of the final migration, they are mainly nocturnal animals and depend to a great extent on an acute sense of smell to find their food. Other eels take this adaptation a great deal further. The nostrils of the leaf-nosed morays of some Indo-Pacific islands are extended into leaf-shaped attachments, giving an exceptionally large surface area for detecting smells. These eels and some 'bearded morays' also have finger-like barbels around the jaws, used as organs of touch.

It is difficult to say clearly what is a true Anguilliform eel and what is not. The exact definition of the order depends on details of the skeletal structure but it is possible to make a reasonable working description which covers most of the characteristics. The body is always long and sinuous. There are no pelvic fins, no spiny rays to the dorsal fin and no conspicuous scales. The tail is pointed, not forked. These rather negative points roughly cover the adults. All species .go through a transparent, leaf-shaped leptocephalus stage. Two other families of fish, quite closely connected to the true eels, also have a leptocephalus larva but these larvae have pelvic fins and forked tails.

EEL-LIKE FISHES

The eel-like body is far from being confined to the members of the Anguilliformes. It had been developed by at least two major groups of fish-like animals in the Ordovician era, before the modern teleost fishes had appeared. These two, still represented by a variety of modern species, are the cephalochordates and the cyclostomes. The lancelet is a cephalochordate. It has no jaws or backbone and the mouth is furnished with a 'beard' of sensory barbels; the dorsal fin extends from head to tail tip. The cyclostome class includes the lampreys, creatures which at first glance look very much like eels in shape and size. They again have neither jaws nor backbone, the mouth being a circular opening.

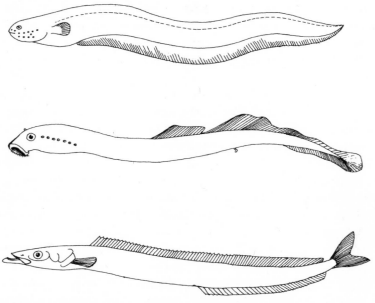

Illus 2 Eel-like fishes: (above) electric eel; (centre) lamprey; (below) sand-eel

In place of the paired gill openings the lampreys have seven pairs and the dorsal fin begins about half way along the back (Illus 2).

Another primitive group has living members which bear a slight resemblance to eels. These are the lung fishes of tropical Africa and South America. Both of these have pelvic fins, to say nothing of profound differences in their internal organisation.

The Brachyopterygians include a single eel-shaped species, the scaly eel of west African waters, readily distinguished by the large scales and dorsal fin replaced by spines.

The division of bony fishes or teleosts, to which the vast majority of modern fishes belong, arose in the Jurassic age and the true eels, as their primitive structure shows, separated themselves at an early stage. There are many other eel-like teleosts and a few may be mentioned here. Perhaps the best known are the electric eels of South American fresh waters. They too are primitive fish but belong to the same order as the carp. The bodies are eel-like and lack pelvic fins but the anal fin is strongly developed and the dorsal completely absent.

Another very important group of fishes is the sand-eel family. These live throughout shallow temperate and cold seas of the northern hemisphere, making a major contribution to the diet of the larger food-fishes. They feed in the surface waters but migrate inshore for spawning and here their slender bodies allow them to burrow quickly and easily in the sand. The sand eels are members of the order Perciformes, which includes the perch, tuna and blennies. They are readily distinguished from the true eels by their forked tails. One of the small, eel-like blennies, the butterfish found on northern seashores has, among other features, pelvic fins.

Finally, three small orders of eels may be mentioned. The first is the Synbranchiformes which are closely related to the Anguilliformes but differ from them in a number of details of structure, including the fusion of the gill openings to make a single opening beneath the throat. Most of the members of the order live in fresh water in tropical Africa and Asia and are capable of surviving for long periods out of the water.

The cuchias of India and Burma have developed a type of lung and spend much of their time in the grass beside ponds. In the water they have to rise to the surface to breathe air. The spiny eels live in fresh water in tropical Africa and south-east Asia and all but one extremely rare species are readily distinguished by the presence of a row of hard spines in front of the dorsal fin. They are predatory, burrowing eels also capable of surviving long periods on the land.

So the eel-like form is shared by many fish and other animals of more or less unrelated anatomical structures. However, nearly all of them have a propensity for burrowing which no doubt was the primary cause of their developing worm-like bodies. This body form conferred another advantage, the ability to move effectively on land, which is an important feature in the lives of some freshwater eels. Perhaps the most remarkable development of the eels has been the ability of the *Anguilla* group to establish themselves as important members of the fish fauna many hundreds of miles from their breeding grounds and at temperatures far colder than those for which their bodies are best adapted.

2

LORE AND LEGEND

In New Zealand the eel-god Tuna had a daughter named Hine who married Maui. Tuna, inadvisedly, would not leave his daughter to take care of herself after the marriage and Maui killed his father-in-law. The severed head of Tuna fled to a river and all freshwater eels are descended from it. Tuna's tail made for the ocean and became the ancestor of the congers.

In a Maori creation myth it was an eel which played the part of the serpent in the Garden of Eden. It seems that any creature of a suitable shape might fit the story. There would have been no freshwater eels in the Garden of Eden and to this day there are no snakes in New Zealand.

But, in the Cook Islands, Tuna benefited mankind by a much more remarkable metamorphosis. It happened this way. The beautiful maiden Ina-moe-aitu once dwelt on the hillside at Tamarua. A slow stream abounding in eels ran near her dwelling and at dawn and at sunset she loved to bathe near a little wood. One day an enormous eel crept up the stream from his hiding place under some rocks. She was frightened at first, but day after day he appeared and after a while began to swim close and touch her. In time she lost her fear and then one glorious evening he changed into a handsome youth. He announced that he was Tuna, god and protector of all eels. Soon he became her lover and they lived together long and happily even though each morning he would change back to his eel form and swim away.

But all love stories come to an end. As his parting token Tuna explained that he must sacrifice himself. He told Ina that the next day he would cause the river to flood so that the waters would come up to her dwelling. He would swim to the door and lay his head on the wooden threshold. She must take an axe, smite off his head and bury it nearby. Then she must water the spot daily. He kept his promise. Ina duly dispatched her lover with one blow and buried the severed head. After a while two shoots appeared and, under Ina's tender care they grew into two coconut palms, the first ever seen on the islands. To this day each coconut bears at its tip the two eyes and mouth of the eel-god Tuna.

This story was set down in 1876 by a missionary, Reverend W. W. Gill, in *Myths and Songs from the South Pacific*. Gill related also that the white kernel of the coconut is called *te roro o Tuna* or 'the brains of Tuna' and in pagan times it was unlawful for women to eat the flesh of the eel. Even in Gill's time most women would refuse to touch it. A 2m eel was caught in 1855 close to the place where Ina-moe-aitu had lived: it was eaten by the Christians but would probably have been treated with greater deference in the old days.

In Tahiti the myth of the eel and the coconut is also told and coconut leaves were used as a talisman to ensure a good day's fishing.

Albert Herre tells that at the foot of the sacred mountain Mugao in the Philippines large sacred eels live in several small lakes. Every day the local children bring them rice and sweet potatoes for which the eels appear to be grateful. The vegetable diet is presumably supplemented by the natural fauna of the lakes. The children sing a song which calls the eels to the feeding place. This is an interesting response, parallel to the carp's recognition of the sound of a dinner bell. In the song the children ask the eels to accept the food and to keep those who offer it free from sickness. Tradition has it that anyone injuring the sacred eels would certainly die, that the springs would dry up and there would be no water for the rice fields.

In Europe the mysteries of the eel led Aristotle to devote a considerable part of his *Natural History* to them. Many of his observations were sound, others understandably vague or incorrect. Congers and morays, he said, had no hard roe and the freshwater eel produced no eggs at all. Those who asserted that they had seen the hair-like young of eels attached to the adults had been careless in their observations, because they had not recorded *where* the supposed young were located. Two thousand years later the great Linnaeus was to repeat the error of believing the eel to be viviparous, and it took the parasitologist Redi to establish that the supposed infant eels were in fact eelworms.

A different species of eelworm, called *Gordius* in honour of the Gordian knot, added to Aristotle's confusion. The *Gordius* or hairworm reaches a length of up to 30cm with a diameter of a millimetre or so. The young live parasitically inside water beetles and other creatures and the adults appear quite suddenly in pools, often in temporary puddles. Hairworms thrash about and wriggle and give a fair impression of an eel-like form. Their way of appearing suddenly in the mud of empty ponds confirmed Aristotle in his belief that eels engendered from the mud itself.

Pliny repeated many of Aristotle's observations but differed in his views on the breeding. Their only way, he asserted, was to rub themselves against rocks after which the scrapings would come to life. He had a great deal more to say, however, on the relationships between the morays and the higher society of Rome. The eels were held in considerable esteem, so much so that channels were cut to allow them to enter inland saltwater ponds convenient to the homes of the Romans where they were well fed and tenderly cared for. One was so beloved by its owner that she presented it with a pair of earrings, perhaps the earliest record of fish-tagging in the literature. The great sizes attained by the freshwater eels of the Indian Ocean were also known to Pliny, but his informants may have exaggerated slightly. In the Ganges, he claimed, eels attain a length of 300ft.

The wonderful eel ball was known to Pliny who described how, when Lake Garda in northern Italy is made rough by the autumn star in October, the eels are massed together by the waves and rolled into a marvellous shoal. Another reference to this is given in Smitt's *Scandinavian Fishes* (1895): 'Frequently the migrating Eel knot themselves together in bunches and large bundles, often a fathom in circumference, are seen lying still in lakes or trundling down the streams.'

One of the few fishery scientists to record eel balls was J. C. Medcof who spent the summer of 1935 watching fish at the outflow of Lake Ainslie in Nova Scotia. On 17 August he saw three spherical clumps of eels, about $\frac{1}{2}$m in diameter, on the bottom of the outflow, as many as thirty in each clump. The eels were knotted together in tight masses which remained motionless amongst the rushes. A fisherman thrust his eel spear into each clump and caught as many as three at a time. At each thrust the eels disentangled themselves immediately and shot off 'like arrows' in all directions. Medcof was told of free-floating eel balls which would sometimes break the surface. It seems that the massing together took place just before the migration of silver eels was due to begin.

Albertus Magnus, the Dominican philosopher and scholar, was born by the Danube in the closing years of the twelfth century. He therefore spent his early years in a land without eels, and it was probably his study of Aristotle which led him to take a great interest in the freshwater eel, though his appointments in Poland and northern Germany may have brought him into contact with the species. He recorded that eels leave the water to feed, a remarkable observation which has been confirmed in modern times. He also told of how, in one exceptionally cold winter, eels left the water and attempted to keep warm by hiding in a haystack. Finally, even there, the frost killed them.

The haystack bed sounds a little unlikely and it would be interesting to have parallel records. The eel's susceptibility to extreme cold, however, has been noticed more recently. William Thompson wrote of how, in February 1841, 'great quantities of this fish, in a dead state, floated down the river Lagan to the quays at Belfast. Here, upon these days, and along the course of the tideway collecting dead eels was quite an occupation at low water, and to the numerous loiterers about the quays proved in some cases more productive for the time than the "chance job" by which they gain their livelihood.' A similar eel kill was recorded in Belfast Lough and in the river Lagan which enters it in 1814. In lakes the winter temperature even under extreme conditions remains high enough to allow torpid eels to survive. Apparently the shallower waters of the Lagan and its estuary reached a lethal temperature more quickly than did the nearby Lough Neagh where the eels survived unharmed. Congers were frozen to death in estuaries in Cork in the south of Ireland in the nineteenth century.

In *Scandinavian Fishes*, Albertus' observations of the eel's behaviour on land are supplemented by those of Bock writing in the eighteenth century :

> This migration explains the mysterious fact that in Prussia and Pomerania fish are caught on dry land and with the plough. On warm nights, when the Eels betake themselves to the peas, the peasants plough a few furrows along the water towards dawn, before the day has broken; and these are the nets in which the Eels are taken. For, though the Eel can drag itself along on the grass, its retreat is cut off by the upturned sods. The rustics consider it a sign of approaching storm when the Eel quits the water for dry land.

Further observations on the eel's liking for green peas were provided by the Dowager Countess of Hamilton early in the nineteenth century. The eels from Lake Hedenlunda wandered into the fields at night and ate pea pods, making a smacking sound with their lips. Close investigation showed that they ate only the soft and juicy outer skin of young pods and did not gnaw through them.

Izaak Walton, writing in the seventeenth century, naturally had a great deal to say about the eel, both from his own acute observations and from his considerable reading. He quotes Francis Bacon's *History of Life and Death* where there is a reference to a 'lamprey' belonging to the Roman Emperor which survived for threescore years, outliving thereby a number of individual emperors. Lamprey in this case refers to an eel, perhaps a freshwater female of longevity approaching Putte's (page 29) or perhaps a moray. This loose use of 'lamprey' makes me wonder whether the unfortunate king Henry I who died of a surfeit of lampreys had in fact over-indulged in eel pie.

Also from the seventeenth century comes an unusual account of eel tagging and recovery in Lough Corrib, which was still spoken of in Thompson's time, nearly 200 years after it happened. Roderic O'Flahertie set it down in 1684:

> From hence [the river Cong] an eele carried a purse of 13s. 4d. sterling, and a knife, for about 16 miles, thro' Lough Orbsen, till it was catched on the river of Galway, which thus happened. One William M'Ghoill, a fisherman at Cong, lighted on a good eele, and, being busie about catching more, thrust his girdle through its guill, which had the purse and knife in it: the eele by chance slides into the river with the purse and knife.

All fishes spawn stories of individuals of colossal size, usually of ones that got away. No eel has beaten Pliny's 100m specimens from the Ganges. The European freshwater eel seems to be one of the smallest of the tribe, the American eel regularly grows much larger while several species from the Indo-Pacific reach lengths of more than 2m. In Ireland 'ten-pound' (4–5kg) eels are quite often mentioned by fishermen but I have yet to see one. The biggest recent specimen weighed over 7lb (3kg) and this was well above the average even for large ones. Thompson saw a 7½ pounder from Lough Neagh. These fine eels are insignificant compared to two specimens from Wisbech in England, described by Leonard Jenyns in or about the 1840s. His notes on Cambridgeshire fishes were published by Alwyne Wheeler in 1973. The eels weighed 28lb and 22lb and one was 6ft long. The record has some credibility since Jenyns was known to be a methodical and well-informed observer and also since a 6ft (1.8m) eel should weigh between 20 and 30lb (9–13kg). The size is also well within the extremes known for the freshwater-eel genus if not for the European species.

Super eels are given full treatment in Bernard Heuvelmans's *In the Wake of the Sea Serpents*. The most tantalising big eel is a marine species, unknown except as a larva. This is the giant leptocephalus. On 31 January 1930 the *Dana*, in the course of the Danish expedition in search of eels, caught a larva approaching 2m in length. It was in the southern Atlantic, between the Cape of Good Hope and St Helena and was swimming at a depth of about 70m. The fully grown larva of a 2m eel measures 6 or 7cm. Simple multiplication suggests that the giant leptocephalus might grow into a genuine sea serpent of 70m or so.

Perhaps it does. If such a monster keeps to deep water the chances against its ever being caught are extremely high. If it surfaces occasionally it will certainly make headline news. Such reports are frequent enough but it seems that, if it really exists, the sea serpent, in common with morays and other large eels, is a shy and retiring beast and likely to stay well clear of humans, their ships and their fishing tackle. I am inclined to accept the existence of many kinds of sea monsters unknown to science as preserved corpses. The failure up to now to capture any specimens of freshwater eels on their very deep breeding grounds is not surprising. If eels of less than 3m cannot be caught in the ocean what chance is there of making contact with a giant? In spite of my inclination to credulity I must add that the simple multiplication sum does not by any means prove the existence of an exceptional adult eel. The giant larva could easily be a case of an individual which failed to change to adult form, or of a species which grows to something approaching its full size while still a larva.

From the transmutation of Tuna to a coconut, to the spontaneous generation of eels from the mud, fantasies abound. Most of them are ancient stories but even modern scientists are capable of making impressive contributions to eel legend. In 1959 the eminently respectable journal *Nature* published an erudite article by D. W. Tucker alleging that the European eel could not and did not breed. He accepted Schmidt's theory that the Sargasso was the place of origin of the young but, on several grounds, held that the Atlantic was too wide for an eel to cross after it has stopped feeding and begun to migrate. The argument was supported by records of the capture of degenerating eels near the coast of Europe; records of the capture of fat, healthy and far from degenerate eels being ignored. The fact that no eels had been captured as adults in the Sargasso was also considered significant.

As the migrating larvae must have some parents the theory suggested that only the American eels, with their much shorter journey to the Sargasso, actually spawned. The fact that no American eels had been captured on the breeding ground was not emphasised. The very considerable differences in the anatomy of the two species were explained by the suggestion that differences in temperature in early development brought about similar changes in other fish. It must be said that all the arguments were well documented and the paper was a most learned piece of work. I was most impressed by it at the time, even though a senior colleague made the sensible remark that such wasteful life cycles were extremely rare.

However, within months of the publication, several eel experts contradicted the theory. In particular their letters pointed out the inconvenient known facts which had been cast aside without comment in the original paper. Certainly Schmidt's classical conclusions do not offer a full and perfect explanation of the migrations of the eel. No scientist has yet produced a total explanation of any phenomenon. Schmidt did offer a reasonable and simple account of a remarkable process. The new theory was neither simple nor logical and required an inordinate amount of special pleading to establish itself. It should have been killed by the subsequent contradictions. But it survived to appear in many text-books and will probably continue to do so. The majority of eel specialists, however, continue to accept the general principles of the Sargasso birthplace, though refinements of the theory will undoubtedly be made.

From fantasy this book now passes to the equally remarkable facts of the lives of eels.

3

FACTS OF LIFE

The common eel of Europe and north Africa is the most intensively studied and commercially the most important of all the Anguilliformes. The arrival of the elvers is a familiar event to fishermen on the lower reaches of rivers. Their presence is shown by the gathering of gulls and other birds which feed avidly on the little eels where waterfalls force them to leave the safety of the deep rivers. Other fishes, including eels, gorge on them. Once I caught in my bare hands an eel of about 500g weight, so intent on her cannibal feast that she ignored my approach. Her stomach containing fifty elvers and she was still hunting.

Often the elver-run passes unnoticed because, when they can, the elvers move under cover of darkness or at least in the shelter of stones and water-weed. The run in Europe may take place as early as February or as late as July, varying from year to year and from place to place. More will be said of it in the next chapter but it is mentioned here because it marks the beginning of the freshwater phase of the eel's life.

After more than two years as an oceanic larva the common eel becomes a fairly sedentary freshwater fish. When the mass movement of elvers has ended, the eel leads a discreet life for some years. It has been caught and cursed from time to time by anglers in search of other quarry. People engaged in preserving salmon waters usually regard it as a dangerous predator. Eel fishermen themselves generally use outlandish gear or fish at night. In Ireland all other fishermen insist that every water abounds in eels and wonder why there is so little interest in catching them.

The end of the eel's sojourn in fresh water is marked by a great migration downstream of eels with large eyes and silvery skins, very different in appearance from the yellow or brownish residents. Between entry and departure the eel feeds and grows. There are two great questions to be asked about this time of the eel's life : what does it eat? How fast does it grow? They are not easy questions to answer. In the first place, eels are usually nocturnal and therefore difficult to observe. Secondly they are rugged individualists.

Fish which live in shoals feed on a few species of abundant organisms. Moreover, they often grow at a steady rate so that a fish of a particular length can be assigned to an age group with a fair degree of accuracy. On the age of the common eel Leon Bertin wrote : 'To judge an eel's age solely by its length would be to risk an error of one to five years either way.' Aristotle had reasonable ideas on the age of the eel, allowing it to live in some cases for 7 or 8 years. Pliny said they lived 8 years. These observations are sound for eels living near the Mediterranean, but rather less than the rule for populations further north. Even 8 years is a considerable length of life for a relatively small fish but this is nothing to the ages which eels may attain. In Ireland specimens of 30 years and over are frequently found while in many waters maturity at less than 15 years old is unusual. The record is held by an eel called Putte. She was caught as an elver in 1863 and therefore presumably born in the Sargasso in 1860. She died in an aquarium in the Museum of Salsingborg in the autumn of 1948, 85 years later.

When individuals vary to this extent, very little information can be gained by examining single specimens. A 60cm eel with a trout in its stomach might be anywhere between 5 and 50 years old and could be a member of a trout-eating population or an exceptional member of a population which normally feeds on invertebrates. The facts of life of an eel population can be determined only by the study of substantial samples.

FOOD AND FEEDING HABITS

Aristotle held that, while some eels fed on mud and scraps thrown to them, the majority subsisted on pure water. Such a situation would make life very simple for a fish culturist, if disheartening for a fisherman. Elsewhere in the *Natural History* he suggested that the diet included eels, grass and roots : the latter two unlikely in a carnivore. Pliny mentioned the fact that they feed at night. In his synopsis on eel biology the Dutch authority, Dr C. L. Deelder, described the eels as 'fully catholic with regard to animal food. A list of species serving as food for eels has to include virtually the whole aquatic fauna (freshwater as well as marine) occurring in the eel's area'.

While it is seldom possible to make direct observations on the habits of eels and, because of their long life-spans, impossible to determine age by marking techniques, two facts help the investigator. The first is that eels normally swallow their food whole. Secondly, in temperate regions, growth ceases completely for some months in winter. This is marked by the formation of 'growth rings' in various bones in the eel's body, so that the age of a specimen can be determined.

The food passes to the stomach where digestion takes place relatively slowly. I made a simple experiment on this by watching three eels which had been captured with full stomachs. They were so full that the shrimps they had eaten could be felt through the skin. After three days at a temperature of 18 °C some food was still undigested. Left to themselves these eels would probably have rested until most of the food had gone and then started out on another foraging expedition.

This slow digestion means that food in the stomach remains easy to identify for a considerable period, at all events long enough to allow for recognition of most of the food organisms if the stomachs are collected the day after the eels have been caught. The 3-day rule is also recognised by eel farmers and fishermen who aim to starve their eels for this period before transporting them. The detailed examination of thousands of

Illus 3 Some of the food organisms from a lake eel of 60cm in length: (above) leech, *Erpobdella*; (centre) shrimp, *Gammarus* and dragonfly nymph, *Enallagma*; (below) caddis larva, *Ocetis*; water louse, *Asellus* and egg mass from the pond snail, *Lymnaea*

eel stomachs has been an important aspect of my research (Illus 3). The variety of food organisms in them confirmed Deelder's dictum on catholicity but it also showed that, while eels do eat just about any animal that will fit in their mouths, they have very strong preferences for particular organisms.

The study of the stomachs also revealed that eels in the wild are far from being the voracious predators that many fish-writers have considered them. About one eel in every three caught in fresh water had an empty stomach and in as many as half of these the hind-gut was empty too. This showed that the eels caught in nets (or sometimes by electrical fishing) had digested their previous meals completely before finding any more food. Presumably those with empty stomachs had been netted in the evening, at the beginning of the night's hunting, before they had actually caught anything.

This is an unusual habit amongst fishes, although well-known in snakes. Freshwater perch and trout, taken at the same time of year as the eels, would normally all have full stomachs. These 'round' fishes, however, live in a state of ceaseless movement, and it is difficult to see how such periodical feeding habits would benefit them. Eels on the other hand usually retire to burrow when resting. There they require very little energy to maintain their positions and they would be far less exposed to the attentions of predators. A single foraging expedition taking place every few days could be a decided advantage.

The stomachs are elastic containers and quite large quantities of food can be packed in. The record in my studies was held by a 950g eel which had eaten another eel and contained 58g of well-digested victim. The prey might have weighed 100g at the time it was swallowed. Another well-fed individual weighed 544g and contained 33g of fish : perch and eel. These figures (for food when swallowed), of the order of 10 per cent of the body weight, are small compared with the capacity of such fish as the pike, which can swallow a trout of about half its own weight. In warm water in fish farms, elvers are fed at the rate of 25 per cent of body weight daily; grown eels at about 10 per cent.

The average weight of food found in eels from Irish lakes was very low, less than 0.1 per cent of the body weight. But the average means little in a case like this since it is depressed by two facts. The first is that many of the eels had empty stomachs. Secondly, some must have been caught at sunset, when they were just beginning to feed and would probably have eaten more if they had had the whole night for hunting.

More than a hundred species of food animals were present in the eels I have caught in fresh water. This was a conservative estimate because some could not be exactly determined, and groups of several species had to be included under single headings. There are considerably fewer species of animals in Ireland than in Britain and fewer in Britain than in mainland Europe, so it is certain that many more than a hundred animal species are eaten by eels. However, while eels may eat almost any small animal that moves, the number of food organisms which play a major part in the diet is much smaller. In Irish lakes only a dozen types were of real importance : ten invertebrates and two fishes, perch and eel.

Details of the food eaten by some of the eel populations studied are given in the Appendix. The variety is impressive but the majority of the animals are kinds which crawl on the bottom. These belong to three principal groups of animals.

The crustaceans include the water fleas of the plankton and a host of shrimp-like creatures as well as the larger crayfish, lobsters and crabs. Planktonic animals by definition are swimmers, but freshwater eels from time to time eat them in enormous numbers. Even the big eels were sometimes found with thousands of tiny water fleas cramming their stomachs. More often the bigger mysids were eaten, especially in deep water. The garden eels of tropical seas are essentially plankton feeders. In Ireland the creeping crustaceans were much more important as eel food than the swimmers, and in some lakes and canals the water lice or pond slaters were the dominant food of eels of all sizes.

Crustaceans spend their entire lives in the water, fresh and salt. Insects are land animals as adults but the larvae of many kinds feed and grow in fresh water where they usually outnumber the crustaceans on the bottom. Insects, however, will not live in sea water. Most of the aquatic insects have a larval life of a year or sometimes two in the water but the winged adults live only for a few days when they mate, lay eggs and die. The larvae of mayflies, caddis flies and above all of the non-biting chironomid midges are eaten by eels. In my studies a diet of chironomids produced the biggest and best eels. Most of the insects eaten by the eels either creep about on water-weed or amongst stones, or anchor themselves to these. The eel's sinuous body allows it to wander amongst dense weed or between

33

stones. The protruding lower lip of the freshwater eels may help them to pick creatures of this type off their supports. I believe that, in general, eels in cool climates thrive because they are able to catch food organisms which the more active 'round' fishes cannot find.

Snails are the third important group of food animals. They belong to the order of molluscs which includes the bivalve shellfishes such as cockles and mussels. My eels kept strictly to relatively small snails. Large species, measuring more than a centimetre or so, were very seldom swallowed even though young specimens of these kinds were eaten. Very small freshwater cockles often appeared in the eel stomachs and in some lakes where other food was scarce they were fairly important. The long lower lip, small mouth and fine teeth of the freshwater eel suggest that these small invertebrates are the food for which it is best suited. But it is one of the most adaptable of fish and the diet is broadened to include many less obvious meals.

One of the most remarkable creatures which I found regularly in eel stomachs was the freshwater mussel. This is quite a large animal with a shell of up to 100mm in length and 30mm deep. The shells are not found in the eel stomachs, but the entire soft bodies occur so frequently in places that they constitute one of the most important sources of food. Unlike the marine mussels the freshwater species are active animals, regularly wandering about with the aid of the fleshy foot which is pushed out between the valves (or halves) of the shell. The eel may be able to grab the foot when it is pushed out and hold on, gradually working its way in and swallowing the whole unfortunate animal.

Large freshwater eels, those above 50cm or so in length, eat fish. In some lakes and rivers they appear to eat nothing else. The favoured victims are perch, small eel and cyprinids such as rudd which are probably the most plentiful species small enough for the predatory eels to manage. In rich lakes in Ireland trout seldom appear in eel stomachs because most of the young trout live in tributary streams and do not reach lakes until well-grown.

In Lough Corrib eels seem to be especially fond of char. The char is quite closely related to the trout, but in Ireland is smaller and normally breeds in lakes so that the young are plentiful there. In places in Lough Corrib it actually seemed that the eels gathered specially to hunt char; exceptionally large numbers of eel were caught in positions where char were numerous. Whitefish, known locally as pollan, powan or vendace, are regarded by long-line fishermen in Lough Neagh and in northern Germany as the best bait for eels.

In Ireland the commercial eel fisheries nearly all depend on the stocks of eels in lakes. My work therefore was concentrated on the lake populations and to date only three rivers have been sampled. Although each of the three is of a distinct chemical type (one acid hill stream, one basic lowland and one intermediate lowland) the feeding habits of the eels are similar in all. They show a marked contrast with the behaviour of lake eels in having more strongly pronounced predatory habits. Lake eels of less than 40cm rarely eat fish and a predominantly fish diet is seldom seen until they are much bigger. In the rivers, fishes are found in the stomachs of eels which are big enough to swallow them, from about 20cm upwards. In their pioneering studies on the food of eels in Welsh rivers, V. R. P. Sinha and J. W. Jones found fish in only a small percentage of their samples. But very few of the eels they caught were large ones.

The fishes eaten by river eels include various members of the carp family, together with small eels, perch, stickleback, pike, salmon, trout and lampreys. A curious discovery I made in the river Erriff was that the eels eat not only the sticklebacks but their nests and eggs as well.

Sport fishermen, concerned with the welfare of salmon and trout, regularly accuse the eel of carrying out the most hideous inroads on their treasured stocks. Sinha and Jones were inclined to think that eels in their rivers did little enough damage and I failed to detect any salmon or trout young in the eels of the Munster Blackwater, one of the finest salmon rivers in Europe. In this case there were a few specimens with fish remains which could not be identified, but all of the recognisable fish proved to be eels or members of the carp family.

There have been well authenticated accounts of eels being seen to swallow salmon eggs at the time of deposition and such stories have led to a supposition (which I have yet to hear proved) that the eels also burrow into salmon redds to devour the eggs. In Lake Windermere, Dr Winifred Frost found eels eating char eggs in winter, perhaps again they snatched them as they were laid. Several facts suggest that the salmon egg-eating habit is unusual. Above all, the great majority of eels are torpid in their burrows in winter at temperatures of less than about 10°C. Salmon and trout rarely spawn at temperatures above 8°C so that very few eels ever come in contact with either the eggs or with the newly hatched fish. What is more, egg-laying salmon are very regularly watched by river wardens and one would expect to have many more records of the unwelcome attendance of eels if this behaviour were at all common. Eels certainly like to eat salmon eggs. A pet eel of mine refused practically any other food but would gorge herself on salmon eggs when they were offered.

In Lake Windermere, Dr Frost found only one fish, a perch, in the stomachs of 100 eels caught by standard methods. On the other hand she examined 70 eels caught in perch traps and found that 34 of these had eaten perch. This and my own observations suggest that eels, while enjoying the diet, find fish difficult to catch. In the open water in lakes the majority of fishes swim above the bottom, out of the eel's reach. In the fast-flowing streams, where fishes rest near the bottom in the slack currents caused by outcropping stones, they would be easier to catch, and in the perch traps the capture of fish would present the eel with no problem at all.

The popularity of fish as bait on long-lines supports the theory that eels like fishes and will eat them where they can easily be caught. Fishes are highly nutritious and a single fish would provide an eel with as much nourishment as a large number of small invertebrates. It should take much less effort on the part of an eel to capture one fish than to secure perhaps hundreds of chironomids. This would suggest that fish-eating eels should be well-fed and fast-growing but the contrary is true. The largely piscivorous eels of the Blackwater in southern Ireland were slow-growing and large-headed, a characteristic associated with poor food. Apparently the difficulty that the eels have in securing fish prey leads to longer periods of starvation between meals and a less well-fed population.

In brackish waters insects become scarce, although in areas of reclaimed land some midge larvae thrive and are eaten in large quantities by the smaller eels. Other small shrimp-like creatures, gammarids and mysids, substitute for the small insects. As the eels grow larger they eat marine shrimps and prawns and a variety of fishes. Small flatfishes such as flounder are swallowed whole and are found tightly rolled up on their long axes in the stomachs. As with the freshwater mussel, the flounders show that the eels have impressive powers of manipulating prey which appears to have an impossible shape. Although lacking the canine teeth of morays and congers, the freshwater eel is clearly equal to the struggle with large items of prey. Another apparently difficult prey species eaten in quantity is the shore crab.

It was not surprising that the feeding habits of eels should vary between the main types of habitats : lakes, rivers, brackish lakes and estuaries. However, within the relatively small area of Ireland and the apparently limited habitat of large, lime-rich lakes studied, the different eel populations showed a remarkable variety of food preferences. It was possible to recognise several distinct types. My sampling had taken place in July or August since a pilot experiment in Lough Corrib had shown that the food eaten did not change noticeably in the course of the two months.

To take a few examples, Lough Corrib eels concentrated on fish and water snails. The Lough Derg and Lough Key populations (most of them large eels which should have been fish-eaters) depended on water lice and bithynia snails with mussels as an important third group. In the Erne lakes where the biggest and best eels lived, chironomids, fish and mysids were the principal food. In this case too, as in Lough Derg, it was particularly interesting to see that small invertebrates rather than fish were the principal diet of eels both big and small. As will be seen these diets give rise to quite distinct populations with regard to rate of growth and size at maturity.

Before leaving the subject of eel food in European waters a few other items may be mentioned. Gunnar Svärdson of Drottningholm wrote of the eel's unwelcome habit of eating the very valuable freshwater crayfish *Astacus* when these were soft and weak after moulting their shells. Indeed Swedish crayfish experts regard eel and crayfish as being incompatible : where eels are plentiful there is not much hope of finding crayfish. The two do exist together in Ireland but only in places where neither is plentiful. The only good crayfish lakes are landlocked ones with no eel population.

Eels show considerable skill in removing and eating fishes which have been immobilised in nets. The evidence for this is strong, though circumstantial. Their readiness to eat immobilised fish is used by the Japanese eel farmers who feed dead fish suspended in the pond water. The eels nibble the flesh away, leaving nothing but heads and bones.

C. L. Deelder describes the extraordinary way in which an eel attacks an object which is too large to swallow : 'The eel bites into the flesh and then tears off the mouthful by rotating around its long axis at high speed.' He also quotes Albertus Magnus : 'The eel allegedly crawls out of the water during the night and enters the fields, where it finds sowed lentils, peas or beans.' It seems more likely that, if this did indeed take place, the eels were hunting for worms or molluscs. Deelder had seen aquarium eels leaving their water to hunt for food. Although fishery biologists do not appear to have reported it, there is a strong country tradition that eels do sometimes hunt on land. It is very unlikely that they would leave the water except after dark in very wet weather and therefore it is not in the least surprising that few people have seen them at it.

38

The most grisly observation concerning the food of eels comes in *The Tin Drum* by Günter Grass, where he describes in loving detail the use of a freshly slaughtered horse's head as an eel trap. Several Baltic-based fishery experts, however, have assured me that this is not a regular method. It does lead to the question of whether eels are scavengers to any great extent. My own observations of the stomach contents point strongly towards a preference for living prey and I have not yet positively identified any stomach contents as offal. Eel fishermen know that bait must be very fresh and long-lines and basket traps have to be cleared and rebaited every day. In the eel farm on the Mosel, deep-frozen fishes are fed to the eels but they must be mixed with fresh blood to make them attractive. Last summer I actually watched an eel in a city park pond eating some dead material. I couldn't make out what, but it was definitely not a normal constituent of the freshwater fauna.

It is well known that eels are plentiful downstream of slaughterhouses and other places where organic waste material is thrown into rivers. These eels may indeed have adopted a diet of dead meat, but it is possible that they gather to prey on chironomids and other insect larvae or worms which would abound in the enriched water. Most probably some wild eels learn to use dead food and, in places where offal is regularly dumped, the Günter Grass technique may work very well.

While the eel in fresh water is mainly a nocturnal animal which feeds at the bottom, there are plenty of exceptions to the rule. One of the most remarkable gatherings I have seen was in a backwater near the bottom of an elver pass at a hydro-electric dam at Ballyshannon. The water was about a metre deep and between 100 and 200 large eels were crowded together at the bottom. Their heads and the first third of their bodies were pointing upwards, swaying a little. Above them the elvers swam and the large eels snapped at any that came close enough.

On the river Shannon where it flows slowly and there is a good growth of weed, eels can be seen at the surface in sunny weather. They appear to be feeding on the larvae of the Simulid black fly which are abundant on the water-weed. Also in sunny weather eels seem to bask in shallow water close to lake shores. They are always watchful and disappear very quickly when a boat comes near. Apparently they are attracted by the warm water.

Information on other species of freshwater eel is less detailed but in general the feeding habits of both temperate and tropical species seem to resemble those of the European, although the sizes reached by mature individuals are different.

It is interesting that in Canadian lakes the brook trout, which is a species of char, is an important item of the eel's diet, an observation comparable to the Lough Corrib eels' feeding habits. Both are cases of salmonids which spawn in lakes. This would make their young readily available to the eels. Also in Canada, J. C. Medcof published some observations of eels in Lake Ainslie, Nova Scotia. They were rarely seen early in the season but, in July, when pond-weeds and waterlilies had grown up, many eels could be seen. Some were looped in inverted Us over the plant stems. Others lay close to the surface but disappeared quickly with a splash when disturbed. By the end of August they were seldom seen.

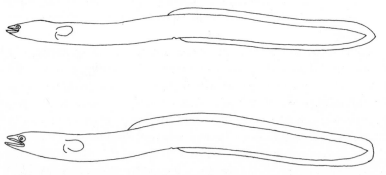

Illus 4 New Zealand freshwater eels: (above) short-finned; (below) long-finned

In New Zealand as many as two-thirds of eel stomachs have been found empty in some studies. D. Cairns worked on both long-finned and short-finned species (Illus 4) and found that, while small specimens of both ate similar food, larger long-finned eels preyed on salmonids to a greater extent than did the short-finned. Both species, however, ate a wide variety of organisms : fish and invertebrates. Possibly the predominance of salmonids in the long-finned was more a reflection of the habitat than an indication of food preferences. It moves further up rivers and might therefore be more likely to come in contact with small enough trout or salmon. A. M. R. Burnet found that, in rivers, trout-eating by long-finned eels began when the eels had reached a length of about 70cm. More trout were eaten in weedy streams than in clean, gravelly ones. Possibly the weed gave the eels better cover from which to snatch the trout unawares.

The overall picture seems to be that eels, whether American, European or Australasian, are not particularly adept in trout-fishing. It was also interesting that the average length of trout eaten by Burnet's large New Zealand eels was only 9cm. No doubt the rather smaller eels of Europe would eat smaller trout. In many game-fish waters trout of these sizes actually need thinning and therefore eel predation might be of no great significance to the salmonid populations.

Little, if anything, is known of the food of the tropical fresh-water eels. Comparison of the feeding habits of eels in, say, the parts of Indonesia where four different species are found would be very interesting. Both the nature of the eels' teeth, fine and rasp-like, and the observations on the stomach contents seem to indicate that *Anguilla* is primarily an invertebrate feeder which in certain cases can adopt a diet of fish.

The feeding habits of the marine eels are not so well known. Species like congers and morays secure their diet of fish to some extent by lying in wait in their tunnels and snapping at victims that pass close enough. The conger, and perhaps the other species, do set out on foraging expeditions. This has been well described by Michael Kennedy :

After sunset, but before full dark, having emerged from the crevices in the pier, they would swim slowly along the fringe of weeds growing on the stone facing of it, snapping at the little pouting, poor cod and pollack which haunt the weeds. As a rule it would be impossible, in the gloom to make out the congers themselves. The disturbance they made by their lazy sinuations through the water would be noticed, however; and when a torch was flashed on, the conger would show like oil streaks weaving in the swell of the tide.

European congers are regularly found in shallow salt water and may move some way up estuaries. They are not so well able to withstand changes in salinity as are freshwater eels. I found that at the mouths of Irish rivers the eel population is largely conger with only a few small freshwater eel present. But further upstream, although the salinity is still relatively high, the freshwater species completely replaces the conger. The conger is virtually unknown in the Baltic although occasional specimens are found off Iceland and northwards along the coast of Norway. The biggest known conger, caught in 1904, measured 270cm and weighed 72kg. Males mature at less than 80cm but females regularly grow to well over 1m. Most or perhaps all forms of fish which the conger can catch are eaten. Michael Kennedy found in a large specimen 5 flat fish, a 5-bearded rockling and 2 crabs. Congers are also on record as having eaten lobster, hake and disabled salmon. Cannibalism and predation on freshwater eels is a normal occurrence. Growth under aquarium conditions may be very fast: 9kg in 2 years, 31kg in 3 years and 40kg in $5\frac{1}{2}$ years have been recorded.

I came to study conger quite by accident and was very surprised to find that I had done so. In the course of the survey of freshwater eels I had chosen a spot at Kilrush, near the mouth of the river Shannon. I had not been able to do the work myself and my assistants had fished and collected a sample of a dozen specimens. Back in the laboratory I was interested to see that many of the supposed freshwater eels were eating hermit crabs but thought little of it. When I came to look at the otoliths I was really struck by the growth pattern – three or four well-defined annual rings appeared where there should have been up to a dozen not so clear ones. Then I noticed that the otoliths were not quite the right shape for a freshwater eel and eventually realised that I had been examining congers. Apparently this was the first time that small congers had been so examined. The following year I collected another sample of congers under similar conditions at Cromane in the south-west of Ireland.

My congers were all caught over a smooth, muddy bottom, a different habitat from the reefs and harbour walls where they usually live. None of the hermit crabs in the stomachs were in their borrowed shells and it seems likely that they were snapped up when searching for larger homes. Shore crabs were another important food item; most of them but not all had soft shells. Shrimps and a variety of small fishes were eaten too.

The most intriguing food animal in the conger stomachs was the freshwater eel. At Cromane the fyke nets caught no freshwater eels and at Kilrush only one. But *small* eels, too small to have been held in the fykes, were found inside the congers. In both cases freshwater eels were plentiful further up the estuaries, in places where the congers could not thrive because of the low salinity. It seems that the two species cannot live together because of the congers' superior powers as a predator.

The eel thrives in fresh water because its nocturnal habits leave it free from the attention of other species of fish. But in salt water the conger, with similar nocturnal habits, keeps its numbers down. Possibly the freshwater eels originally left their natural saltwater habitat as a result of pressure from the more successful marine families. Fisheries for freshwater eels in the sea exist mainly north of the congers' range, while the principal fisheries for European eels are not in fresh water but in lagoons of too low salinity for congers.

The conger eats more and in much larger portions than the freshwater eels. While I have never found a freshwater eel containing food of more than 6 per cent of its body weight, figures for the congers were regularly up to 7 or 8 per cent. Nearly all of the stomachs of my congers contained food and clearly they were much more efficient and active hunters. Their growth rates were relatively high : 5 year olds averaged 1–3kg. This is still low by the standards of other fishes in the same regions. A salmon in a single year at sea grows as much as a conger in five. As in the case of the freshwater eel, the conger in temperate waters seems to be far outside its ancestral range.

It seems likely that the eels of coral reefs in general follow the habits of the congers. A close study, however, would not be likely to show identical habits amongst all species. The fact that in the tropics many species of more or less closely related eels are found close together is evidence that there *must* be differences in food and habits between each – otherwise a single species would have taken over the habitat.

A number of eels have highly specialised ways of feeding. One of the most picturesque is the garden eel which lives in sand down to a depth of 30m in many tropical seas. They are small, less than 30cm with long, narrow nearly cylindrical bodies, very small upward-pointing mouths and relatively enormous eyes. The hind nostrils are slits and the front pair very small so that it seems that these eels rely on sight much more than scent or touch to capture their prey of small planktonic animals. Their behaviour is beautifully described by Cousteau in *Life and Death in a Coral Sea*. They live in shoals but each member has a separate burrow. They keep their tails in the burrows and extend their bodies above the sand, heads facing into the current where they search for food organisms. When danger threatens they spring back into the burrows, disappearing completely until they consider the coast is clear again. Then, inch by inch they creep out and resume their interrupted meal. When the garden eel retires it plugs the mouth of its burrow with mucus which presumably protects it from any predator which might try to dig it out.

The extent of the powers of escape of these eels has been shown graphically by various divers. In the 1930s William Beebe tried to dislodge them by every known method including a large charge of dynamite. The Cousteau approach was more gentle and eventually succeeded. His team used an anaesthetic, MS222. They first injected it into the burrows with a view to putting the eels to sleep so that they could be sucked out. This also failed because of the efficiency of the mucus plug. They then tried covering a few of the burrows with plexiglass domes and introducing the anaesthetic to these enclosures. This scheme worked well. The eels after a while emerged from their burrows into the drugged water and fell gently asleep.

Morays have a reputation for being aggressive and likely to attack humans. Certainly they can be dangerous, a bite from their strong jaws and sharp teeth is hardly likely to be pleasant. It is also true that an eel, safely retired into a rock crevice, has a distinct advantage and will maintain its position. If a careless diver puts his hand into the mouth of a moray, or perhaps even very close to it, the chances are that the eel will snap and hold him firmly, conceivably with fatal results. This kind of behaviour is a long way from 'aggressive' and it seems that a truer picture of the situation is that the morays are in reality retiring creatures, preferring to lie up in their lairs, disguised both from prey and predators by their spotted or barred colour patterns. Cousteau's diving crews have experienced considerable difficulty in inducing these great eels to leave their hiding places. By treating them gently the divers were able to induce the morays to feed from their hands. Small morays feed on crabs. Above a length of 40cm they turn to a diet of fish.

Deep-sea eels such as the snipe eels and thread eels generally have large eyes which must be of some help to them even in the gloom of the abyssal water. Many of them, however, are also well endowed with large pores on the head and lateral lines which presumably have sensory connections and can feel the slight disturbances in the water as a shrimp or some other small animal passes. Some of these eels have elastic stomachs and an arrangement of bones in the skull which allows the swallowing of large objects. It is amazing to see the stomach of a slender and delicate eel bulging with one or two large, well-armoured and robust shrimps. Perhaps the very fact that the eels are 'loosely' constructed makes them equal to the struggles of the less supple crustaceans. From time to time these small and long-beaked eels have been collected with larger fishes, and the suggestion has been made that they use their forceps-like beaks to take parasites from the skins of the large fishes. I have found sea lice from salmon in the stomachs of freshwater eels and have often wondered whether they were nibbled off a passing salmon. But they may have been picked up from the bed of the lake.

The slime eels are more or less parasitic, living on larger fishes such as halibut. They attack by biting and nibbling away at the flesh, presumably the strong tongue is used as a rasp. They show an interesting case of parallel evolution with the cyclostome hagfish. Both forms have developed the round mouth and strong tongue suitable for burrowing into fish flesh. What is more, both are capable of producing immense quantities of slime. According to Bigelow and Schroder : 'We may add from experience that it is as slimy as a hag and drips with sheets of mucus when drawn out of the water.' This excessive sliminess is a protective device, shielding the parasite from the digestive juices of the prey and possibly also making it distasteful. A specimen of slime eel recently placed in the British Museum (Natural History) was caught in water 1,300m deep off the south-west coast of Ireland by Dr A. McDonald who was attempting to catch hagfish at the time.

EEL AGE

Whatever the eel eats, it grows : older, longer and heavier. The determination of the age of eels is a fine art, with a fair degree of science combined. Growth rings, resulting from the alternating periods of fast and slow growth in the life of temperate fish, are found in many parts of the skeleton. The problem is to find a structure which can be examined conveniently. Scales are the most popular since they can easily be scraped off the body and storage and subsequent examination are simple.

Until 1913 eel scales, which show quite clear annual rings, were used for the purpose; but E. Ehrenbaum and H. Marukawa of Hamburg pointed out that, in the common eel, scales do not even begin to develop until the individual is about 6 years old. To make matters more complicated, the scales continue to be laid down for several years. So a sample of scales tells very little. You must add six to the number of rings and even then cannot be certain that the collection included the oldest scales on the specimen. Besides this difficulty many of the marine eels have no scales.

Ehrenbaum and Marukawa established the use of the otolith in eel age determination. In life it is part of the balancing organ which tells the fish when it is on an even keel. It hangs in a fluid-filled chamber at the base of the skull so that, when the eel rolls or pitches, the otolith moves towards what is temporarily the lowest part of the chamber. The otoliths are roughly oval and range in size from about $\frac{1}{2}$mm in length in elvers to about 5mm in large adults.

The annual rings of small otoliths can be seen clearly through a low-power microscope with the otolith immersed in creosote. Those from eels of more than 30cm or so in length are more difficult, and the traditional treatment was to grind one side away. This is rather tedious and, fortunately, in 1964 J. Moeller Christensen of the Danish Fishery Institute described a simpler technique of examining burned otoliths, which he used in a study of soles. This works very well for eels and, in Dublin, Trevor Champ made a detailed study of otoliths in which he compared the two methods, concluding that the burning technique gave results closely comparable with the grinding method and made the rings very much more easily read in the case of specimens of more than about 12 years old. Eels as old as this were not so important in the intensively fished European waters where the greater part of eel population studies had been made. But in Ireland the majority of eels in my samples were older than 12 and it was essential to have a simple way of determining their ages.

Illus 5   Otolith of 11 year old eel – a 'clear' otolith indicating rapid and even growth throughout life

In places where the eels are well fed and grow at a steady rate in the warmer part of the year, they produce otoliths which are very easy to interpret. Broad white bands of material deposited in the summer are separated by charred black winter rings (Illus 5). In Ireland such eels are rather uncommon and the otoliths show signs of periods of cessation of growth in summer, so that there are more rings than the eel has years. Generally speaking the winter rings are blacker and more distinct than the additional summer 'checks'.

The interpretation of difficult otoliths is a job for an experienced worker. Perhaps twenty or thirty eels in a sample of a hundred will have easily read otoliths. The remainder will be more or less complicated but, with practice, it becomes possible in most cases to decide which rings are annual and which should be ignored. The determination is seldom absolutely certain, but the results are accurate enough to provide an invaluable aid to population studies.

In 1975 an international working party on determining the ages of eels was organised by the European Inland Fisheries Advisory Commission. Considerable disagreement on how to interpret the otoliths was achieved in a friendly manner. One of the outcomes of the meeting was to arrange for the supply of otoliths from eels whose ages were actually known. I found that my readings of burned otoliths tended to underestimate the ages slightly, but still gave a reasonably accurate result.

Besides the European eels I applied the burning technique to congers and to two species of freshwater eel from Malagasy. The congers were very easy to read and had grown about twice the rate of the freshwater ones which lived close by. The Malagasy specimens were difficult. Presumably these eels feed in warm water throughout the year and do not show any very clear winter resting period. The specimens had measured about 60cm and seemed to be 4 or 5 years old.

GROWTH RATES

The determination of the ages of fish is probably the most important single aspect of fisheries (though not necessarily of fish) biology. When the age composition – the proportions of fish of each age – is known, it is relatively easy to decide whether too many or too few eels are being caught or whether the intensity of fishing is just right. The reading of thousands of otoliths of Irish eels showed in particular that there were several distinct populations in the country.

In the first category come the splendid eels of the lakes of the Erne system. They had long been known to the fishermen as exceptionally fine ones and it had been believed that they owed their size simply to being rather small in numbers and therefore uncrowned. It turned out, however, that eels were more plentiful there than in some lakes where the usual catch was of much smaller specimens. The age determinations showed that the Erne eels are big because they grow faster than usual. What is more, the Erne eels reach maturity at an early age by

Irish standards, specimens of more than 12 years old being very scarce while the majority were 8 or 9 years.

In other lakes where food is plentiful and the eels grow more slowly, silver eels of different sizes may be found. For example the silvers are small in Lough Corrib and large in the Shannon. Apparently the Corrib eels reach maturity at an earlier age, before they have time to grow as large as the Shannon population. Where the food supply is poor the eels grow more slowly and take more time to mature.

Presumably these differences in growth rate and age at maturity depend on the nature of the food. My results suggested, but tentatively, that a diet of fish and insect larvae resulted in rapid growth and early maturity. Slow growth with early maturity was caused by a diet of molluscs and fish, while slow growth and late maturity came from a largely invertebrate diet. Unfortunately, similarly detailed studies of food and growth rate have not been made elsewhere and no evidence is available to confirm or discount my theory.

Apart from the practical considerations (in showing how potentially good eel lakes may be distinguished from others) the results were interesting in showing that the growth rate is only partly controlled by temperature and some aspects of water chemistry. In the lakes in my study both the alkalinity of the water and the temperatures could be taken as constant factors. Alkalinity in many cases is a very good guide to fish productivity, but it seems that in the case of eels some more subtle factors are operating. It will be seen, however, that in warmer countries growth of eels is very much more rapid than in Ireland, and there is every reason to believe that the temperature can limit the rate of growth.

Very old eels are found quite often. In 1973 an unusually large silver eel, 103cm in length and over 2kg weight from the river Shannon was found to be 30 years old. It has sometimes been suggested that some eels stay permanently in fresh water and never attain the migrating stage. This would be hard to disprove, but it seems quite likely that all eels eventually mature

50

and it is significant that this 30 year old was caught on migration. Even Putte (page 29) had become silver when she died at 85. In Scotland Gordon Williamson has determined ages of up to 50 in the wild.

A very interesting big eel was caught in 1974 in an enclosed pond called 'The Lough' in the city of Cork in the south of Ireland. She measured well over 1m and weighed 3½kg. She was 20 years old but had almost stopped growing by 13. The otolith showed that growth had been rapid up to that age but in the last seven years the rings were very close together. It seems likely that she had tried to migrate at 13 years and, after failing to escape, returned to her home for another year, trying again each winter.

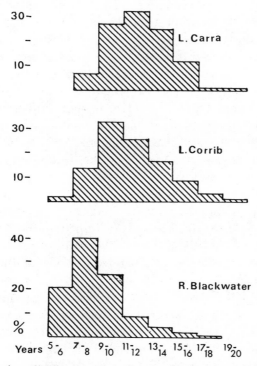

Illus 6 Age distribution of freshwater eels from estuary (Blackwater), downstream lake (Corrib) and upstream lake (Carra)

Some details of age determinations from a number of Irish waters are given in Illus 6. They show several interesting features. Eels of over 12 years are comparatively scarce in brackish water, certainly more so than in most of the lakes. Young eels are much more plentiful in these waters, while in the furthest upstream lakes such as Carra, eels of less than 9 years old are uncommon. This supports the theory that eels take many years to ascend rivers. While they reach the highest points of rivers in as small a country as Ireland they are completely absent from the upper waters of the great rivers of Europe, unless they have been planted artificially.

Growth rates of the same order as those of the Irish eels have been found by other workers in northern Europe. In 1966 Jorgen Dahl of the Danish Fisheries Institute caused some consternation by reporting growth rates bearing no relationship to these. He had stocked disused carp ponds with eels which reached an average of over 40cm after three years (as opposed to about ten years). For a while it looked as if the traditional methods of age determination would have to be questioned, but it transpired that the eels in question had grown at an abnormally high speed. The old fish ponds would have been exceptionally rich in invertebrate life and, to allow for the carp to breed, must have maintained a temperature of over 20°C for several weeks each year.

Another case of rapid growth is that of the eels of Lake Ferto in Hungary. As in other eastern European lakes there were no naturally occurring eels. Elvers were introduced in 1963 and, by 1969, mature eels with an average weight of 600g were caught. In this case the average summer temperature of the water is about 26°C. I was sent some otoliths of younger eels from a similar lake. They showed four clear black winter rings, each of them separated by about three indistinct 'checks', showing brief cessations of growth in the course of each summer. Eels in Greece grow at a similar rate and reach large sizes. The connection between temperature and rate of growth is not completely straightforward. Deelder gives the example of eels he studied from the Neretva delta in Yugoslavia, where he found both fast and slow growing specimens. It does seem very unlikely, however, that any normal eels can grow really quickly in places where the temperature stays below 20°C. In laboratory experiments in Denmark, Jan and Inge Boëtius discovered that the eel's respiratory and heart rates were at their highest at 25°C to 26°C, and no doubt these temperatures under natural conditions would allow the best possible use of available food leading to the highest growth rates.

In Canada Donal A. Hurley examined 1,500 eels from Lake Ontario and the Ottawa river, and his paper provides some of the most useful data on American eel populations. The eels in Lake Ontario grew nearly twice as fast as northern European specimens and a similar growth rate was found in Newfoundland. In the Ottawa river, growth was much slower. The fast growth rate of the Lake Ontario eels led to their attaining the large sizes known for the American species. Specimens of over 10 years old average more than 70cm and at 15 years they are approaching 1m. These eels show just the same enormous variation between individuals that is known in Europe. The oldest eel in Hurley's sample was 19 years.

In New Zealand, where two species of freshwater eel have been studied, the short-finned live mainly in lagoons, lakes and slow-flowing rivers. The long-finned are found in these still waters but also in fast-flowing rivers and are therefore more widely distributed. The long-finned are nearly half as heavy again as short-finned of the same length. Figures are provided by D. Cairns in a paper published in 1941 which also provides details on the growth rate. The short-finned increase faster in length, but mature more rapidly and migrate at a lower average length than the long-finned.

New Zealand eels of both species seldom migrate at less than 12 years and Professor Peter Castle believes that most of them are considerably older. Although the growth rates of these eels is faster than the Atlantic species it is still well below the average for other New Zealand fish, once again suggesting that the eels of temperate countries are living in water which is too cold for them.

The examination of samples of dead eels leads to conclusions as to their feeding and rate of growth. Information on the habits of normal, healthy and free eels is very much harder to come by and much of it is a matter of speculation. It is hard enough to come to firm conclusions on the behaviour of fishes which are active in daylight. But the common eel usually lies up in a burrow or a crevice until dusk so that direct observations can seldom be made. However, by studying the size and distribution of catches and by occasional chance observations in the day-time much can be told of the way of life of the eel.

The summer fyke nets (page 114) which are set to catch feeding eels depend on certain habits of the victims. Very few eels are caught in these nets in the daytime since most (but by no means all) of the eels are resting. Whatever time of the day the nets are used it is apparent that an eel, wandering over the lake or river bed in search of food, follows the leader net when it meets it. This, of course, leads the eel into one of the traps. In still water I have found roughly equal numbers of eels in each trap, showing that they have no particular preference for swimming into deeper or shallower water. Clearly they are not in the least upset by the net and don't discover that anything is wrong until too late. Other species of fish seldom behave in this way and in lakes the fykes catch very few of them. Presumably when they meet the obstruction of the net they either turn away or swim over it.

As a beginner fishing in estuaries, I made great efforts to stretch my nets across the current, on the assumption that the eels were swimming up and down the river bed rather than from side to side. This proved so difficult to manage and it was so much easier to set the nets with the current that I changed my technique and caught just as many.

All through one summer season my assistants, Ann Fortune and Tina Royle, set a train of fyke nets in one position in Lough Key. On 4 July, the first day, 18 eels were caught. The total catch for the next 7 days was 19, and only 12 eels were caught in the course of 7 weeks after that. The inference was that one night's fishing would remove about half the eels from an area and the population would be reduced to very small proportions after 8 days fishing. What was more, in the course of the later summer, few eels returned to the area. They were back again in numbers in the following April.

Quite a different pattern showed in the Blackwater estuary where I ran a similar experiment. Here a smaller train of nets caught 5 eels on the first day, 22 on the second and the catch remained relatively high for 10 days. It fell for some weeks and the experiment stopped for a while in mid-July. When the nets were next set, 3 weeks later, they made a catch of 99 eels, followed by another low period of several weeks and one more rise at the end of August. So the estuarine eels clearly wander over a far wider range in their foraging trips. In the estuary of the river Slaney fishermen get good results throughout the season by fishing in the one place.

A rather surprising discovery in the Blackwater was that the eels seldom feed above the level of low tide. This fact led to disappointments in my very first experiments when I set the nets over the tidal mud and came back on the following low tide to find innumerable shore crabs but very few eels. Later on I found that eels are scarce in broad regions of the estuary, where large areas of mud are left exposed, and much more plentiful in narrow reaches where the water flows between steep banks. It is difficult to know why this should be the case, since both birds and such fishes as bass and flounder find plenty of food over the tidal flats. In some other estuaries fishermen do make reasonable catches between the tides.

Facts of Life

POPULATION DENSITIES

There are two views on the density of eel populations. Trout men will assure you that there are thousands of eels in any given stretch of water. On the other hand eel fishermen, past or present, will insist that eels are very scarce now, though they can remember much better times. Neither view is particularly helpful. The lack of information is not at all surprising when the difficulties of catching and counting eels are considered. I was lucky enough to get figures from two completely unfished eel haunts. One is a peculiar area, the 'channel' of an area of reclaimed land, the South Sloblands of Wexford. This is something of a miniature IJsselmeer and, when I began my investigations in 1970, proved to contain the most abundant eels of my experience. I had set enough nets to catch, by normal standards, twenty or thirty eels – just enough for my assistants to examine in the course of a day's work. We caught several hundred each time. The following year commercial eel fishing was tried there and yielded over $1\frac{1}{2}$ tonnes. This represented some 9,000 eels of over 40cm length and must have removed a high proportion of the stock – the following year's fishing yielded only about 200kg. The area of the water was 75ha from which a density of 1 eel to 80sq metres is calculated. This, of course, takes no account of the numbers of smaller eels, averaging 7 years old and less, which must have been present in greater numbers.

The second area was part of the river Blackwater at about 1m deep, a slow lowland river some 50m wide. Fishing with fyke nets for 3 nights in the same stretch yielded three eels of over 40cm to 100sq metres. There must, of course, have been many smaller eels in the area so that these figures cannot be compared directly with estimates which are based on small eels. The South Sloblands and Blackwater stocks were between 5 and 10 times as dense as those found in other Irish waters.

In the IJsselmeer, B. Havinga reckoned that the density of eels was 9 per sq metre. B. J. Muus calculated that between 1 and

10 eels could be found in 20sq metres of Danish fjords where the vegetation was dense. Both these figures refer to stocks from which most of the bigger eels have been removed by fishing. Had the large eels been present they might have led to a higher number of individuals to the square metre, or they might have reduced the numbers by preying on the smaller specimens.

About half of the catch of American eels is made in Canada and most of the research on the species has been carried out there. M. W. Smith and J. W. Saunders were able to provide figures for the standing crops of eels for lakes in which all the fish had been poisoned by rotenone. Eels react quickly to this poison and may actually leave the water when it is applied. Even so it is possible that a proportion of the victims reacted to poisoning by burying themselves and, whether they died or not, avoided collection. The largest crop found in this investigation was in Bill's Lake, New Brunswick, where there was 1 eel to 19sq metres.

Probably the greatest numbers of eels in Europe are to be found in the lagoons beside the Mediterranean shores. These lagoons are shallow and the water warm so that the production of food organisms is very high. Unfortunately much of the fishing is operated on a free for all basis and many of the eels caught and sold are no bigger than pencils. It is interesting that the biggest European producers of 'freshwater' eels – Denmark, Italy and France – all depend on salt or brackish-water stocks rather than on freshwater populations.

SEX DETERMINATION

The density of population leads to the vexed question of the sexuality of freshwater eels, since males are more plentiful in dense populations and females in spare ones. Some observations have not been disputed. The sex can rarely be determined until a length of 20cm has been attained, and it is very often difficult to distinguish the sexes in specimens of 30cm and more. To add to the difficulties, Sinha and Jones found female cells in the course of microscopic examination of developing male organs. One of the few simple facts of the matter is that the male silver eels are rarely more than 47cm in length and females seldom less. In the upper waters of great rivers like the Rhine, where the population is thin, male eels are unknown, and the same is true in the upstream lakes of Ireland – unless, as in Lough Neagh and the Shannon system, elvers have been artificially introduced. In estuaries the percentage of females is very much lower though in estuaries in Ireland where no eel fishing takes place female eels are still plentiful. Long-line or fyke-net fishing for feeding eels would naturally tend to select the females, since many males migrate before growing big enough to be caught.

The problem of sexing young eels is of more than academic interest. Elvers are expensive both to capture and to transport to the upper reaches of river systems. If sex is determined at birth, then half any consignment of elvers will be males which can be expected to reach maturity and migrate as small fish of considerably less value than the larger females. An eel-fishery owner would give a lot to be able to buy females. But the problems seem likely to prove even more difficult than those concerning the breeding of the eel, since under natural conditions in temperate Europe it takes five to ten years for an eel to reach a size at which its sex may be easily recognised.

The effect of density of population on sex determination has been mentioned by several authorities: as already mentioned, dense eel stocks are largely males, at low densities females preponderate. There are at least two possible explanations for this. M. Fidora actually made a series of experimental stockings at different concentrations of eels, and found more males developing in the most crowded populations. He concluded from this that density did affect sex determination. His results undoubtedly supported this idea and the observed facts in nature do point in this direction. The other theory, however, is not disproved by the experiments. Let us assume that the potential proportions of male and female are equal.

There are profound differences in the physiology of male and female eels and therefore there is reason to believe that their habits are inherently different. Females grow bigger and migrate further upstream. Supposing that even when very small the females are more active, they will tend to wander further from the crowd in search of the greater quantities of food that they must need. They may be less well adapted to living in crowded conditions than the less active males. If for some reason females are forced to live in a crowd they would be subjected to greater stresses than the more sociable males. This might lead to serious debilitation of the females, followed by their being weakened and falling an easy prey to the healthier males.

This alternative theory is as attractive as the more widely accepted idea that some outside factors act on the germ cells to induce determination towards male or female according to the circumstances. It possibly explains better the observation that the overland transport of elvers to places such as Lough Neagh in Ireland results in an increase in the proportion of males in the catches of silver eels. I find it hard to believe that planting elvers in such a large lake, which is very intensively fished for yellow eels, could give rise to conditions sufficiently crowded to induce the change of sex.

Controlled experiments to resolve the case are extremely difficult to make. First of all the duration of the experiment is a major problem. Few biologists have the opportunity to run a project which requires from ten to fifteen years unbroken attention. The time could be reduced by using warm water and feeding at a high rate, but these are just the kinds of factors which could influence the sex ratios. Then there is the matter of space. It is all very well to keep a hundred elvers in a glass tank but each one will grow to anything from 30cm to 50cm in length before the experiment can be concluded and that makes a serious problem. Some brave investigators have actually embarked on these projects.

4

WANDERINGS

The migrations of the freshwater eel are amongst the most remarkable of animal journeys. Although much effort has been devoted to studying the journeys little is actually known, but that little makes an extremely interesting story.

We begin with the arrival of elvers and their movement upstream, since this is one of the more familiar stages of the migration and visible to anyone who visits suitable places at the right season. Thereafter the nature of the migratory movements are known only to specialists and a major part of the journey, back across the ocean to the breeding place, is still a matter for speculation.

ELVERS

Round about Christmas the first elvers reach the coasts of Europe. They are transparent and therefore known as 'glass eels'. Later on pigment develops and they become greyish or black in colour. As long as the water is cold the glass eels stay in salt water but increasing temperature leads to changes in their behaviour. At Den Oever in Holland, where the water from the IJsselmeer flows through sluices to the Wadden Sea, elvers are never seen until the temperature has risen to 4.5 °C or more. Movement into the rivers and upstream is delayed for considerably longer and needs a temperature of 9 °C to begin.

Between the time of their arrival in inshore waters and their entry to fresh water, a period of a month or so, the elvers undergo a dramatic series of changes in behaviour, which were

Illus 7   European 'glass-eel', length 6.5cm

studied in detail by Deelder in the 1950s. At the beginning of this 'transition period' when the elvers first arrive in the estuary, they apparently keep to deeper water and also avoid close contact with each other. Some days later they begin to be seen at the surface and have a tendency to congregate, at which stage they may be seen in great shoals, swimming in harmony. They are repelled by bright light, diving down into the water to get away from it, but attracted by a weak light. As time goes on they begin to be attracted by a strong light and in fresh water are often seen migrating in broad daylight.

Another gradual change is in their reaction to fresh water. Newly arrived elvers keep well clear of it and try to escape when they are placed in it. This behaviour has completely changed

61

by the end of a month at which time they show no tendency to escape. At the Ardnacrusha dam on the river Shannon in Ireland, there is a fish-pass leading from the freshwater headrace down to tidal water below, bypassing the turbines of the generating station. Elvers there, according to Donal O'Leary, arrive in February but usually wait until May or June before entering the fish-pass. Here the urge to move upstream is probably connected with temperature as well as with the time taken for the behavioural change. The change may be to some extent a slow physiological adaptation, allowing the sea-going elvers to develop the necessary mechanism for thriving in fresh water. The body fluids of freshwater fish contain a higher concentration of salt than is found in the surrounding water. Because of this there is a tendency for water from outside to enter the fish through the skin and especially through the gills. All fish therefore have a mechanism which regulates the uptake of water and maintains a balance. Saltwater fish on the other hand live in a medium which has a higher salt concentration than their body fluids and the regulating mechanism is completely different since its function is to prevent water from leaving the fish.

The great majority of fish live wholly in fresh water or in the sea and cannot ever change from one to the other. But apparently eels which live in estuaries and silver eels migrating to the sea can adapt themselves quickly. It seems reasonable to suppose that glass eels which have never been exposed to fresh water would take some time to develop the ability to adapt.

When the transition period is over and the elvers have finally lost their abhorrence of fresh water they move on into water of decreasing salinity. The obvious conclusion to be drawn is that they are now influenced by a direct urge to get away from the salt. However, F. Creutzberg of the zoological station at Den Helder (quite close to the IJsselmeer dam) came to totally different conclusions. He has shown that the incoming elvers were able to distinguish between ebb and flood tides and used the tide streams to bring them towards the land. They allowed themselves to be carried by the flood tide but swam to shelter on the bottom so that they would not be taken back by the ebb.

When he began to study elver behaviour in an aquarium, he found that the elvers actually moved *away* from inflowing fresh water, preferring the salt water which they should have been ready to leave. They behaved normally when canal water rather than the aquarium water was used. The explanation was that the aquarium fresh water had passed through a charcoal filter which apparently removed some aromatic compound which attracted the eels. So the elvers were drawn towards the smell of fresh water rather than being repelled by the taste of salt.

Once the migration from salt to fresh water (or at least from sea to estuarine conditions) has begun, the elvers use the banks of the river to guide them. They can feel their passage parallel to the bank as far as a metre away from it. This can lead them into trouble under certain circumstances, and Deelder described the unhappy event of elvers getting shut in a canal lock and swimming round and round it. In another situation some of the elvers which had come to the top of an elver ladder turned to follow a dam across the river instead of going on along the bank. This led them into a strong current which swept them downstream again.

Frequently, great numbers of elvers in early spring wait in the estuaries, held back only by low water temperatures. As soon as the minimum temperature for immigration is reached immense hordes of the baby eels come in together. Their desire to swim within a metre or so of the river banks concentrates them even more; so that the phenomenon of a black stream of elvers on the move has been recorded many times. It is believed in Germany that the greatest movements take place when high tide occurs round about midnight. The reason seems to be that activity increases after sunset and therefore the elvers using the tide stream to carry them would have a few hours in which to travel. Indeed, eels seem to have a predilection for the first few hours of dusk : they use this period in infancy, in feeding and when returning to the ocean. However, the elver migration is often seen in progress in the daytime. Possibly this occurs when low temperatures have persisted rather later than usual and the urge to move upstream conquers the desire to use the cover of darkness.

This daylight migration must surely be a little abnormal since it exposes the elvers to the attentions of a great variety of predators, especially gulls of several species, to say nothing of trout and other fishes, most of which hunt in daylight. At night the most dangerous predator is the larger eel and the elvers' habit of migrating on the surface may have evolved to avoid the unwelcome attention of their ancestors at this stage. The urge to press forwards is remarkably strong. Elvers which reach a dead end or have been trapped for sale readily leave the water and can climb for several inches up vertical concrete or wood, provided it is damp. At waterfalls, where the flow is far too strong for them, they again leave the main stream and wriggle through the damp mosses which cover the stones where the

Illus 8 Migrating eels, young and old, can travel out of the water provided they can keep moist. Elvers in bright sunshine are shown climbing up damp moss on a vertical waterfall

water splashes (Illus 8). Elver traps and passes depend on the fact that the elvers are attracted by weak currents.

It is difficult to tell how far upstream the active migration of the elvers goes on. In Holland migration at the surface has been seen 120km from the sea, but in water still under the influence of the tide. Probably the rather headlong rush comes to an end within a few kilometres of the highest point of the tide, and increasing numbers of elvers drop away from the school to begin to feed and adopt the individualistic habits which they will keep for the next few years. The elver trap at Ardnacrusha on the river Shannon in Ireland leads up from tidal water and catches nothing but elvers in their first spring after metamorphosis. A similar trap at Parteen, 15km upstream, takes few or possibly no elvers, but quantities of older and larger eels. The great concentrations of elvers seem to be typical of coastal or estuarine regions, or of rivers fairly close to them.

YELLOW-EEL MIGRATIONS

The mass migration of the elvers may continue for some months; it is often in progress as late as July in Ireland. At some stage during the summer the elvers begin to feed and can be said to enter the 'yellow-eel' stage. Male eels seldom move very far from the estuary or from the lower regions of rivers, but a great many of the females continue to travel upstream throughout their lives.

This movement is accompanied by an unknown degree of migration downstream, usually in the autumn. Yellow eels are captured in small numbers in the silver-eel nets. In the Blackwater estuary and in Lough Corrib, the waters which I studied extensively outside the months of July and August, eels of more than 40cm length were noticeably scarcer in May than in the later months. This could be explained by supposing that the bigger eels drop downstream for some distance in autumn and move gradually back again after the winter.

The return migration is easier to observe and there are many records of yellow eels moving upstream through fish-passes. In 1963 H. Mann noticed that eels on the Elbe, most of them between 17 and 22cm, began to move upstream when the temperature reached 8 or 9°C. The intensity of migration increased a great deal at higher temperatures, up to 22°C. At an elver trap on the river Shannon at Parteen weir, a sample of eels which I examined contained individuals of up to 10 years of age. No doubt older ones would have been found if the trap could have caught them. At this trap in June half the catch was 1 or 2 years old and the rest older. Although the trap was only 15km upstream from the tide, elvers rarely reached it in their first year.

Yellow-eel migration has been studied in many parts of Europe. In the Baltic there is a slow, gradual movement away from the Atlantic, and Deelder compiled a table from work done by various experts in the early years of the century. In Trollhättan, near Göteborg, the average age of a sample was 3.7 years and length 25.7cm. Near Norrköping the age was 5.5 years and length 30.4cm, and at Alvkarleby, some way north of Uppsala, the age was 6.3 years and length 36.2cm (Illus 9).

In this connection Friedrich-Wilhelm Tesch's tagging experiments in the North Sea are especially interesting. His eels showed remarkable powers of homing, some of them getting back after being released up to 180km away. What was really remarkable about the homing was the speed of the eels, which could be up to 3km per hour. Now, the distance from Norrköping to Alvkarleby is about 400km and eels take about one 6-month season to cover it. A displaced eel, however, in a hurry to get home, might cover the distance in a week.

In New Brunswick Professor V. Vladykov carried out transplanting experiments on the American eel, taking a collection of them by motor car over a distance of about 50km. Rather than moving them from one place to another in the open sea, these eels were taken from one river to another, which would have made homing much more difficult. Four out of a total of fifteen recaptures were made from the home stream, but the

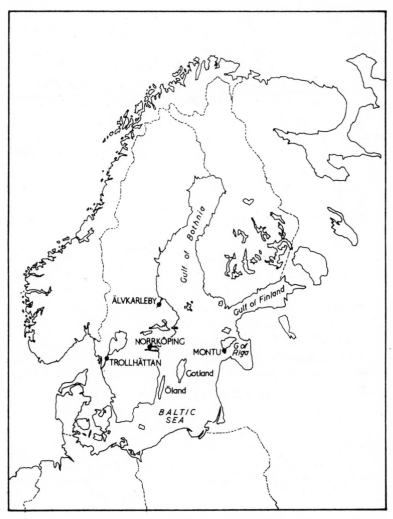

Illus 9 Baltic region. Silver eels tagged in Gulfs of Finland and Riga have been recovered at Montu, Gotland and Öland

majority stayed near the point of release. The homing in this case was amazing, since it required the eels to move first downstream and then southwards when their instincts should have encouraged them to go in the opposite directions.

It seems that, although the eels normally make a leisurely ascent of their river or passage through an area like the Baltic (which is more of an estuary than a sea), they have a strong urge to travel back to a region they had grown familiar with. So they make a much more positive effort to return than they did on their first journey. In this way eels which had migrated downstream for the winter might be expected to make a quick return journey to the point they had reached the previous summer. Then they could resume their gentler upstream wanderings.

In 1974 Tesch published the results of experiments in tracking individual yellow eels, two from the Elbe estuary and two from Gdingen in Poland. These were tagged with ultrasonic transmitters and followed by boat from a point of release near Heligoland. They moved generally in an easterly direction, in contrast to silver eels which in the same experiment swam northwest. The experiments indicated clearly the eel's ability to steer a compass course. They also suggested the possibility of the eel accurately remembering its previous route, allowing it to make a rapid trip home. These powers will be mentioned again in connection with the migration of the silver eels.

Finally, the most remarkable of all the yellow eels' wanderings deserves to be mentioned. Country tradition has it that they can discover the nearest water when released on land. E. Schaffer in 1919 reported on his experiments in the Stockholm region which proved their ability beyond any doubt. Eels were able to travel to water over distances of several hundred metres, even over hills and against the wind – apparently ruling out influence of slope and scent.

SILVER EELS

The extent of the migration of yellow eels is unknown. As far as can be judged by the sizes and ages of eels in lakes and even in estuaries, many individuals settle down at an early age and make no attempt to go far upstream. On the other hand, great numbers travel towards the higher parts of the river systems throughout their lives. In the St Lawrence in Canada and in some of the great rivers of east Africa, eels are found trying to surmount dams hundreds of kilometres from the sea. On the St Lawrence these eels may be 60cm and more; lengths at which European eels are more likely to be preparing for their final spawning migration downstream.

Whether the eels are sedentary creatures or inveterate wanderers, they finally reach the maturing stage when they cease feeding and change to the 'silver-eel' form. The eyes grow bigger and the skin colour changes from brown to a blackish or purple shade on the upper parts shading to whitish or silver below. The feel of the body changes too. Yellow eels have soft bellies but the flesh of the silvers is much firmer so that it is difficult to squeeze the sides of the body cavity together. Internally the sex organs can usually be seen to be quite well developed, male and female being easy to distinguish.

These changes indicate that the eels are ready to set off on the final migratory journey of their lives. The factors which bring on the changes are not clearly understood. It is well-known that silver eels have much more fat in their bodies than do the yellows. Possibly when sufficient fat has been accumulated (the aim of the female eel, according to Fritz Thurow, is to contain 28 per cent of fat), preparations for the migration begin. This still does not answer the question of why female European eels rarely, if ever, become silver at a length of less than 45cm but may attain any length between that and over 1m, whereas the males very seldom grow to more than 45cm and may be as small as 31cm. Male American eels, according to Vladykov, are smaller. The longest he examined was only 37.5cm. The proportion of fat in the body may be decisive, but that simply raises the question as to why some eels use their food to grow in length instead of directing it to the production of fat. I believe the exact nature of the diet influences this.

The migrations of the silver eels begin in autumn and the time of the greatest 'runs' is closely connected with weather conditions and with the phases of the moon. Clearly, the eels prefer to move under cover of darkness and in turbid water. So there is no normal migration in the daytime nor on bright moonlight nights when the water is clear. Few fishermen even bother to set their nets at the time of full moon unless the rivers are in spate. On the other hand there is very little migration when the rivers are low, even on dark nights.

The greatest level of activity happens if flood conditions occur fairly early in the autumn. A few nights of high water in September or October may be enough for the greater part of a population of silver eels to leave an area of fresh water. On the other hand, if no substantial floods take place before the end of December there may be no significant migration until the new year and possibly not until early summer. However, like the feeding eels, the migrants are individualists and there is always a trickle of migration throughout the autumn, some individuals being overcome by the urge to travel even under unsuitable conditions.

The study of the behaviour of silver eels is exceptionally difficult. They rest in the daytime and they avoid bright lights at night so direct observation is hardly ever possible. The one incontrovertible fact is that the migration is a downstream movement which brings the eels to the sea. In rivers this appears to be a straightforward case of swimming with the flow, and it seems that eels are capable of appreciating the direction of the greatly reduced water currents in lakes. In this part of their journey the wind exerts a strong influence, probably indirectly by influencing the direction of the current. In Lough Neagh, where the outflow is on the north side, a strong southerly wind causes an increased eel run. In Lough Corrib, which flows towards the south-west, a north-easterly wind is considered the best. In the IJsselmeer where eels are caught in fyke nets on both sides, relatively more eels are caught on the eastern side when the wind is from the west. Similar observations have been made in the Baltic.

Finally, at the river mouth or the entry of a lagoon to the

sea, salt water appears to attract the silver eels. As the whole
point of the migration is to bring the eels to their breeding
grounds in the ocean, this is scarcely surprising. It is interesting,
though, in showing how the chemical stimulus of the salt overrides the physical one of the current. Fishermen believe that the
eels, which up till then have been swimming with the river
current, will reverse their behaviour and swim against an
inflowing current of salt water.

A few direct observations have been made on the behaviour
of silver eels. In the field, R. H. Lowe in England saw silver
eels in a brook, where they swam head-first downstream along
the bottom. C. L. Deelder watched silver eels at night in a
large aquarium and 'was astonished by their apparent clumsiness.
With slow snake-like movements, their round pectorals wide-
spread, they seemed to "glide" lazily through the water, giving
the impression that all movements are fulfilled with as small
an effort as possible.' These observations need a good deal of
qualification. It does seem reasonable that the migrating eels
put the minimum of effort into their swimming – they have a
very long journey and must make the best of their food reserves.
However, the nature of the traps used by fishermen show that
the swimming is far from passive or blundering and also that
many eels travel in the mid-water, well above the river bed.

Yellow eels in lakes can be caught easily by using low walls
of netting (of the order of 50cm high) to guide them into traps.
These nets catch few silver eels. For them the equivalent trap is
a large 'pound net' whose guide wall must stand above the
surface of the water. Apparently, while the yellow eels are
content to follow an obstruction along the bottom, the silvers
react by trying to swim over it.

In the headrace to the Ardnacrusha generating station in
Ireland, Donal O'Leary placed nets at different levels in the
water to find out where the eels were swimming. The basis of
this experiment was a practical one. Since the water in the
headrace was needed to generate electricity the eel catch was a
matter of secondary importance, and the fishermen were not

allowed to block the headrace completely with their nets since this would have reduced the flow to the turbines too much. What made the results particularly interesting from the biological point of view was that the headrace was a straight, artificial channel and the rate of flow over the whole cross-section was much more constant than in a normal river. In the headrace the eels tended to travel on the bottom when their numbers were small. On the nights of the big runs, however, they swam at all levels and apparently were fairly evenly distributed through the water. Indeed, some silver-eel fisheries, including several on the Elbe, depend entirely on eels which swim above the bottom, since the net is supported at the surface and does not extend all the way to the river bed.

The inefficiency of silver-eel traps is an impressive tribute to the eel's ability to avoid obstacles. In 1960 I made a simple experiment on the Kells Blackwater river in Ireland. Most of the eels caught on this river come from a lake upstream of the traps. A number of silver eels caught on the river were tagged and brought back to the lake. In the course of the next week 64 tagged eels were recaptured: none at the trap nearest the lake, 49 at the next, 9km downstream, and 9 at the lowest, 3km farther down. That amounted to only 10 per cent of the number of eels tagged, but complications had arisen which prevented us from saying that the three traps caught only 10 per cent of the eel run. In the first place an unknown number of eels lost their tags. The second snag was much more interesting: two tagged eels were recaptured the following year. The interruption of the journey had so upset their plans for migration that they gave up and took a year to come back to normal. Very similar results, both as to trap inefficiency and captured eels taking a year before moving on again, came from experiments in the river Shannon.

Whatever may be done artificially to halt the silver eel's passage, a number of natural happenings regularly delay the journey. Above all, the coming of daylight brings the movement to an end. In Germany it is considered that migration normally begins with sunset and ends at midnight. This observation is hardly universal, for in many Irish rivers on the nights of heavy eel runs the movement continues throughout the hours of darkness; though when the runs are light it is true that few eels are caught after the first few hours.

These facts suggest that the migrating eels prefer to keep a certain distance apart from each other. Suppose that they try to swim on the bottom and aim to make about an hour's journey in the course of the night. When the migrant population is well spread out, as it might be in long rivers where there are few lakes or none at all, the eels can fulfil both these desires without any overcrowding. The Irish fisheries, however, are nearly all situated at short distances, less than 20km, downstream of lakes. In these cases a dense population will wish to go through a narrow constriction as they leave the lake on a particularly favourable night. There will not be room for them all to swim on the bottom, nor will they all be able to travel together in the course of the first hour or so of darkness. If the strongest urge is to travel for an hour every night, and this overrides the urges to travel at sunset and on the bottom, then the migration is bound to take place throughout the night and at all levels if the river cannot accommodate the eels in any other way.

The idea of the eels' jostling each other in their haste to leave a lake for a river presupposes that they have congregated close to the outflow of the lake to await favourable conditions for moving on. In England R. H. Lowe was able to demonstrate this by trapping experiments. Winifred Frost mentioned that this habit in Lough Neagh enables fishermen to catch the eels by seine net. Unfortunately in the latter case the fishing was illegal, and close observations could not be made. There are similar clandestine fisheries in other waters.

The presence of lakes on a river system seems to have a profound effect on the silver eels. Deelder gave figures for a Dutch lake, the Amstelmeer, which showed that eels entering the lake from a canal were mostly caught in August while the majority leaving the lake were not seen until October. Apparently the lake delayed the eels migrating from upstream by a period of two months. It also seems that the lake eels themselves did not even begin to leave until two months later than the eels in the canal upstream. This and similar observations show that migration from shallow water takes place earlier than from deep.

This might be explained by supposing that a sharp increase in the flow of the water is enough to send the eels on their way early in the season. In shallow waters such an increase would be very distinct. The delaying influence of a lake such as the Amstelmeer can be understood by remembering that the canal eels were acting under the influence of a pronounced current which would have disappeared quite suddenly on entry to the lake. It is reasonable to imagine that such eels could take some time to readjust their sensitivity to the water flow. This delay could also explain why some of my tagged silver eels were so thoroughly upset that they took a year to make their way onwards.

The influence of the moon on migration seems to be rather more than a matter of the eels avoiding bright light. All over northern Europe scientists and fishermen have found that the peak runs tend to take place round about the last quarter of the moon. This is the time when the early part of the night is dark and coincides with the eel's preference for moving soon after sunset. Deelder and other scientists have studied the matter in rather greater depth, showing that the connection is not entirely straightforward. Even when nights are so cloudy that the intensity of light of the moon is masked, the eels still show an attachment to the time of the last quarter. In the Upper Rhine the peak runs happen just before the last quarter, while in Holland and the Baltic the greatest movement is observed after it.

Deelder suggests that in the course of their lives the eels are continually influenced by the moon so that a recognition of its rhythm is assimilated by them. This could be so strong that, when migration time comes, the light intensity no longer affects them but the time is easily recognised. The slight difference in lunar time favoured by the Upper Rhine eels may be connected with their sex. In the Upper Rhine all of the eels are female, while in Holland and the Baltic males are present in equal numbers or may even preponderate.

A very remarkable stimulus for a mass migration of silver eels, suggested by Deelder in 1954, is microseismic activity. The only constant factor that he could discover in twenty-eight peak eel runs over six years was an atmospheric depression in the vicinity. The local weather at the place of migration had not always explained the run. The microseisms are miniscule earth tremors, probably set up by the influence of high waves at sea in the centre of the depression. The only sharp rises in the eel catches took place after the occurrence of microseisms with a 3-second period, caused by depressions over the North Sea and the English Channel. The pressure fluctuations in water which these microseisms would cause are of the order of 0.002 millibars. Deelder goes on to point out that, if the microseisms do explain the eel activity, then silver eels in captivity should become restless at the appropriate times. Apparently the connection has not been fully studied, but both practical fishermen and biologists have noticed that captive silver eels show increased activity at the times when the peak runs are happening outside. Some fishermen, indeed, keep a few captives under observation to get a forecast of when the wild eels will begin to run in numbers.

The capture of silver eels in the open sea is so difficult that it is rarely tried, and there is therefore very little information on how they behave when the influence of rivers can no longer be felt. One exception exists in the case of the Baltic and Deelder, who besides his expertise on eels has carried out research on bird migration, gives an invaluable review of the situation there in his *Synopsis*. He bases his theory mainly on the results of A. Maar who tagged silver eels in the Gulfs of Finland and Riga in the eastern Baltic in the late 1930s. These eels apparently more or less followed the coast as far as Montu and then set off across the sea towards the south-west (Illus 9). Hardly any were recovered on the east or south coasts but many turned up on Gotland, Öland and the Swedish coast. If the coastal movement had been followed there should have been no recoveries from these points.

Now, if the eels had aimed to make the shortest possible journey to the Sargasso from the Gulf of Finland they should have set out in a direction a little to the north-west, to follow the great circle route. If they had been influenced by hydrographic conditions they would not have cut across the sea in the direction they chose. It appears therefore that they tended all the time to move to the south-west and followed the coast only when it actually blocked their chosen paths. The interesting thing about the direction taken by the Baltic eels is that it fits well with the bearing of the Sargasso Sea (W 30° S) so that by keeping to this line the eels should come to within reach of their spawning area.

At least three mechanisms for direction findings are known. C. G. Edelstam in Sweden in 1965 showed in tank experiments that silver eels are capable of steering by the stars. He then tried out the abilities of eels in the field, by releasing them with long-stringed rubber balloons attached. Within a short time after release nearly all of them would head off in the same direction, although it often took a few minutes of random swimming to allow them to come to a decision. However, the direction could be found correctly on overcast days, which suggests that the star navigation was not being used at that stage whatever happened subsequently.

Deelder referred to a chance observation of eels migrating at night in the Great Belt (the sea channel between the Danish islands of Fünen and Zealand). They were spotted by a ship's searchlight, swimming close to the surface and certainly able to see the stars. Deelder also makes the point that the white belly of the silver eel is typical of a fish which swims near the surface; deep-sea fish usually are uniformly coloured. It is therefore likely that swimming close to the surface by night is normal behaviour for migrating eels in the early stages of their sea journey.

Secondly, some migrating animals are able to travel on a course determined by their keeping to a particular angle to the direction of the earth's magnetic field. F.-W. Tesch's experiments in tracking individual eels with an ultrasonic tag led him to favour this theory. His eels in the North Sea took a north-north-west course which would bring them to the Atlantic by a route between Scotland and Norway rather than through the English Channel. The eels which he followed swam quickly and with relatively little wandering. The adoption of the straight course supports the idea that a magnetic influence is dominating the eels.

Thirdly, there is the very interesting fact that eels are extremely sensitive to electric fields. This was demonstrated in the laboratory in 1972 by S. A. Rommel jr and J. D. McCleave in the University of Maine and similar experiments were made about the same time by N. A. Mikhailenko in the Institute of Biology of South Seas in Sevastopol. Eels were shown to be sensitive enough to be able to determine the direction of a water current. This, as the discoverers pointed out, does not mean that eels have been proved to use electric fields for direction finding but the fact that they *could* do so is interesting enough.

Using pressure-sensitive ultrasonic transmitters, Stasko and Rommel tracked five migrating eels in the sea off New Brunswick in the autumn of 1973. These eels spent much of their time diving to the bottom and swimming to near the surface. Each one would swim for hours at a time near the surface, but none stayed long in deep water. The authors suggested that the diving might be a means of sampling the water-current-generated electric fields which are strongest near the surface and near the bottom.

Supposing that eels leave the waters of the Continental Shelf by sidereal or geomagnetic navigation they still have to find their way against the current of the Gulf Stream to the Sargasso. In the darkness of deep ocean waters a fish has no known means of telling the direction of a current unless the electrical field can be felt. River fish can maintain their positions relative to the land either by seeing or feeling nearby physical features, but ocean dwellers have no such points of reference.

The existence of three effective mechanisms for orientation is not surprising. Blind human beings can lead long and healthy lives, but this does not suggest that sight is not used by the human race. The search for a single direction-finding mechanism in a fish or any other migrating animal is pointless and has an unfortunate tendency to steer investigators away from the more interesting problem of how the various stimuli interact.

However they reach the ocean, it seems that the silver eels change their appearance once more. On rare occasions migrating eels which showed signs of an advanced state of development have been captured. Descriptions of such eels have been published by Gunnar Svärdson in 1949 and C. J. Rasmussen in 1951. These eels had very large eyes, pointed pectoral fins and a bronze colour. The pointed pectorals are characteristic of fast-swimming fishes of the open sea while the large eyes (which have much in common with the eyes of the conger and some deep-sea eels) together with the darker belly, are deep-sea features. Since a considerable proportion of the eels of the world are deep-sea fish it seems reasonable to expect a return to this habitat by the migrating freshwater species.

Having shown how eels might find their way across the ocean, the question of whether they have the speed and stamina for the journey remains. A. Maar made the record of the fastest known eel – it travelled at 62.8km per day, followed by one at 54.5km; while as long ago as 1908 F. Trybom and G. Schneider had established speeds of up to 50km a day. In these experiments average speeds were substantially lower but, in measuring the speed of a fish by tagging experiments, the high rates are the only really meaningful ones. Presumably the 'fastest' individuals are those which recovered rapidly from the tagging and made their ways directly to the place of recovery, being recorded there soon after arrival. Speeds which appear slower must be explained to some extent by the possibility first of the specimen's taking a while to recover and find its proper path, and secondly to the likelihood that it was actually caught many hours before the tag was noticed. Tesch's North-Sea eels swam at speeds approaching 2km per hour.

At speeds of this order the Atlantic crossing might be made in eighty days or so, an interesting figure because it gives an eel leaving western Europe up to the end of November comfortable time to reach the Sargasso for the spawning season in February. It is also a relatively short period for a fish to migrate on an empty stomach. For example, the Atlantic salmon in Ireland regularly fasts for ten months or more before spawning.

Sooner or later one or more European eels will be captured on their spawning grounds, so completing the known facts of the life cycle. It is not at all surprising that none have yet been found there. The slippery eel is notoriously difficult to catch by any conventional fishing method. Bait has little attraction for a fasting eel and the chances of a stationary trap catching eels at great depths in mid-ocean are remote.

To sum up, it might then be taken that the eels, once free of the influence of the rivers they grew up in, find their way westward by a combination of navigation by the stars and by maintaining a constant angle to the earth's magnetic field. At a later stage they leave the surface waters and in the open ocean, where no barriers to their progress exist, they head into the Gulf Stream with the aid of their electrical senses.

These possibilities have been demonstrated by experiment. The final stage of the journey is a matter of informed guesswork since no adult eels have ever been caught in the vicinity of the Sargasso Sea. Possibly they find their final destination by their sense of smell – just as the elvers used this to locate freshwater streams. Having arrived there, it is believed that spawning takes place at depths of 100–200m where the temperature in winter is about 20°C.

LARVAL EELS

Having thus tactfully passed over the mating and spawning of the European eel, the facts of the life history can be resumed at the stage of the very young larvae. Deelder stated that the smallest larvae on record were found by the Danish research vessel *Dana* in the course of cruises in 1966. No larvae at all were found in February of that year but in April small ones were plentiful in the south-western part of the area in which Schmidt had found somewhat larger ones. E. Bertelsen who described the capture, concluded that spawning had taken place in March. The area lies close to where the Tropic of Cancer crosses the line of 60° W longitude.

Bertelsen's discovery was a refinement of the major results of the studies of Johannes Schmidt of the Danish Commission for Investigation of the Sea. Schmidt had been engaged in studying the breeding places of gadoid (cod family) fish in the Atlantic, a project which entailed capturing and examining large numbers of young fish from the surface waters. In 1904, eight years after Grassi and Calandruccio (page 12) had shown that the fish then called *Leptocephalus brevirostris* was the larva of the eel, Schmidt happened to find a specimen of it in the Atlantic. This chance discovery led to his famous detailed investigation. In 1922 Schmidt published an account of his results in the *Philosophical Transactions* of the Royal Society of London. The same august body, incidentally, had published the discovery of Grassi and Calandruccio in 1896. Schmidt's Royal Society paper is a superb piece of scientific writing and deserves reading in full. His account of the beginning of the study and his conclusions are quoted here:

In May, 1904, after towing a Petersen's young-fish trawl near the surface of the water, west of the Faroes, it was found, on examining the contents of the net, that in addition to various other forms of pelagic life, we had also captured a specimen of *Leptocephalus brevirostris*, $7\frac{1}{2}$ cm. long.

Thus the larva of the eel was for the first time found outside the Mediterranean. And the find, which was followed in the same year by another, made by Mr. Farran from the S.S. Helga off the West Coast of Ireland, afforded a starting point for future investigations. Owing to various circumstances it came about that Denmark, a country where eel fishing is a specially important industry, was accorded the task of prosecuting the investigation farther, and it fell to my lot to take charge of the work . . .

The system Schmidt used was the one he had established in tracing the breeding grounds of other fish. Numerous samples were collected in tow nets, the individual young fish were measured and, of course, the places and times of capture were recorded. The cruises of investigation ranged from America to Egypt and from Iceland to the Canary Islands. They were carried out mainly by Danish research vessels, but important contributions were made by merchant ships which obligingly made plankton hauls in some regions on their regular voyages.

As the work progressed the journey of the larvae was mapped in more and more detail, based on the observations that, within certain areas, all larvae were below a given size. The 1922 paper was illustrated by a sort of a contour map which has since appeared in innumerable zoology text-books. The 'contours' showing the lengths of larvae centre on the Sargasso Sea. Schmidt's map also shows the distribution of leptocephali of the American eel, distinguished from the European species by the vertebral counts. While his search of the ocean was in progress Schmidt and his helpers also studied samples of eels from all over their European and north African range. He concluded that all these eels belonged to a single species, further evidence that the Sargasso region was the sole spawning ground.

Eighteen years after the start of the work Schmidt drew the following conclusions about the early life of the eel :

Spawning commences in early spring, lasting to well on in summer. The tiny larvae, 7–15 mm long, float in water-layers about 200–300 metres from the surface, in a temperature of about 20°C. The larvae grow rapidly during their first months, and in their first summer average about 25 mm in length . . . They now move up into the uppermost water-layers, the great majority being found between 50 and 25 metres, or at times even at the surface itself. Then they commence their journey towards the shores of Europe, aided by the eastward movement of the surface water itself. During their first summer, they are to be found in the western Atlantic (west of 50° long. W.). By their second summer they have attained an average length of 50–55 mm, and the bulk are now in the central Atlantic. By the third summer, they have arrived off the coastal banks of Europe, and are now full-grown, averaging about 75 mm in length, but still retaining the compressed, leaf-shaped larval form. In the course of the autumn and winter, they undergo the retrograde metamorphosis which gives them their shape as eels and brings them to the elver stage, in which they move into the shores and make their way up rivers and watercourses everywhere.

So, after a period of about $2\frac{1}{2}$ years, the larvae have reached the offshore waters, and at 3 years of age the little eels are making their ways upstream. The leptocephali, transparent and leaf-like, thus appear to be passive migrants to some extent, carried by the Gulf Stream and the North Atlantic Current. This explains the great concentration of elvers in south-western Europe. The fact that the direction of the currents shifts from year to year accounts for the abundance of elvers in some seasons and their scarcity in others. Recent work by F.-W. Tesch and others has shown that the numbers of leptocephali fluctuate enormously from year to year. Successive sampling cruises revealed ten times as many in one season compared with the next.

The distribution of the elvers, however, is far from being a simple matter. This was first brought home to me when I discovered that eels were comparatively scarce in the river systems of the west of Ireland. It had always been assumed that, on account of the closeness of the west coast of Ireland to the Gulf Stream, elvers must be abundant in the rivers. Studies on the relative abundance of eels in various lakes and river systems in the country made it all too clear that the western lakes were very much under-stocked with eels and the only explanation seemed to be that elvers were relatively few. On the other hand, the English river Severn, far from the Gulf Stream, is renowned for its enormous run of elvers.

Another curious aspect is the length of time taken by the larvae to make their crossing. A floating object can cross the Atlantic from Florida Strait to Great Britain in as little as ten months and there are records of 1 year old Mexican turtles being found in British waters. If the leptocephali simply drifted with the current they should not take anything like $2\frac{1}{2}$ years to complete the journey. One possible explanation is that the elvers are carried away from the Sargasso in spite of themselves. They might recognise the direction of the current by their electrical sensitivity already mentioned (p 78) and swim against it.

In considering the long time taken by the migrating larvae it is also important to remember that the Atlantic was not always as wide as it is now. Eel fossils have been found as far back as the Cretaceous, showing that eels were well established at that time. It is quite conceivable therefore that the Atlantic freshwater eels once made relatively short journeys to their feeding grounds and slowly developed the abnormally long larval life which they now show.

Whatever happens on the way across, it is clear that the larvae can maintain their positions at least at the end of the journey. This happens when they reach the edge of the Continental Shelf where the water is about 1,000m deep. Here they stay and go through their first metamorphosis, from leptocephalus to the round, thread-like elver or 'glass eel', so called on account of its transparency. In the course of this metamorphosis the infant eel grows shorter and loses a considerable amount of weight.

They stay in the region of the 1,000m line for some time until the metamorphosis is complete. How they know they have reached the region is far from certain, but Deelder has suggested that the larvae can recognise the position by their sensitivity to low-frequency resonance. This is caused primarily by the waves at the surface sending vibrations down to the bottom. The period of the resonance would depend on the depth, yet another example of the eel's extreme sensitivity to changing pressure.

After metamorphosis the elvers continue their journey eastwards. They take no food on the way and in the course of the next year decrease in length and weight so that late-arriving elvers are considerably shorter than the early ones, perhaps by as much as a centimetre or 15 per cent of their full length, Alternatively, it is possible that the small size of late elvers is evidence of later arrival offshore of smaller individual larvae. Whatever the precise facts may be, the elvers arrive in the rivers and the cycle is completed.

OTHER FRESHWATER EELS AND THEIR DISTRIBUTION

The distribution of the freshwater eels is closely connected with their migratory habits. It seems to be essential that they have access to a spawning ground where the water is warm, about 20°C, at considerable depths, perhaps 200m. Such conditions are far from common in the oceans and so the spawning places are few. To bring the larvae from their birthplace to coastal areas strong ocean currents are required. The absence of suitable currents crossing the Pacific explains the fact that there are no freshwater eels whatever on the Pacific coast of the Americas.

Five eels, including the European species, travel to temperate countries. The remaining ten are tropical and all clearly share a point of origin between the Indian and Pacific Oceans. There is no good reason to doubt that the temperate eels came originally from the same region. The records of eels thousands of miles outside their normal range are particularly interesting in this connection. *Anguilla anguilla* has strayed from the Atlantic to the east coast of Africa, *A. rostrata* has been found in Greenland and *A. obscura* in south Africa. The fact that these strays have actually been seen by man in the twentieth century is evidence that, in terms of geological time, the wanderings are frequent events. There is therefore no great difficulty in explaining the existence of widely scattered eel populations.

Perhaps some such chance migration led to the establishment of an eel population in the Atlantic. Possibly the two Atlantic species arose from two Indo-Pacific ancestors. Otherwise one ancestor could have given rise to the two populations. This problem may be solved as more sophisticated methods of separating species of animals come available.

Before leaving the European eel, the variations in form which it shows must be mentioned. On the grounds of these variations many so-called 'species' were described in the nineteenth century. The principal varieties are the 'broad-nosed' and the 'narrow-nosed'. The former has a large head and rather thin body – the specimen in Illus 1 clearly belongs to this type. The latter is much more slender and has a pointed snout. Fritz Thurow took measurements of large samples of German eels and showed that, while there were many extreme cases which could be distinguished as broad or narrow, the majority were intermediate and there was continuous variation from one extreme to the other.

The second Atlantic eel is the American eel, *A. rostrata*. Like the European species it breeds in the region of the Sargasso Sea and is not found south of the equator. The American eel has a much shorter journey to the mainland and takes only one year for its larval travels. American eels are plentiful in Canada, where the elvers arrive in spring in vast numbers. They are common in the northern United States but become scarcer towards the south. They have been recorded in most of the countries north of the equator but the main population definitely belongs to the temperate parts of the continent. As in the case of the European eels, the American kind has every appearance of being a single undivided species with only one breeding place (Illus 10).

In the Pacific only one species is found in north temperate regions. This is the Japanese eel, *Anguilla japonica*, which closely resembles the American in its life cycle and is the basis of important fisheries. It was assumed for a long time that the larvae of the Japanese eel matured in ten months but, after long study of the matter, Professor Isao Matsui recently concluded that the time taken is still uncertain. Small larvae have been collected to the south-east of Okinawa in February. Large specimens and metamorphosing larvae were found to the east of Taiwan by the research vessel *Hakuho-Maru* in November 1973. This vessel, belonging to the University of Tokyo, has been concentrating on hunting for leptocephali and perhaps will finally succeed in discovering this eel's breeding place.

A second species of eel is found in Japanese waters but is known only in the south and is of little importance compared with the valuable *A. japonica*. This is a mottled eel, *A. marmorata* which reaches a length of more than $1\frac{1}{2}$m. *A. marmorata* has the widest distribution of all of the freshwater eels. Its range extends from the east coast of Africa and the island of Malagasy to the Indo-Pacific islands and across to the Marquesas. Three separate races of *A. marmorata* have been described, indicating the existence of at least three distinct breeding places.

The two temperate eels which live in New Zealand have already been mentioned (page 41): the short-finned *A. australis* (sub-species *schmidti*) and the long-finned *A. dieffenbachi*. They follow the general pattern of migrating seawards in autumn, but an interesting feature of the migration is that the two species appear to leave at different times and sometimes the males have been recorded as leaving before the females. This earlier migration of males would be a reasonable phenomenon. Small fish swim more slowly than large individuals of the same species and, as they must both be present at the spawning grounds together, the males could be expected to begin the journey earlier. New Zealand eel larvae have seldom been found: no more than two, both short-finned, have been identified with certainty. On the evidence of the directions of ocean currents, Castle believes that breeding takes place between Fiji and Tahiti. A very useful summary of the biology of the New Zealand eels was published in 1974 by W. Skrsynski.

In Australia four species of eel are known. One is a sub-species of the New Zealand short-finned: *Anguilla australis*

australis and enters the rivers of New South Wales, Tasmania and Victoria. Like the New Zealand race these eels reach considerable sizes, over 1m in length, and weigh at least 11kg. They are believed to breed in a region close to that of the New Zealand eels, but the fact that there is a recognisable sub-species would indicate that the spawning places are not precisely the same. The Tasman Sea is a possible breeding ground.

On the north-east coast of Australia the long-finned plain coloured eel *Anguilla bicolor bicolor* has been collected from Beagle Bay and Roebuck Bay. However it seems to be only an occasional visitor there and belongs properly to the islands to the north. Similarly *Anguilla obscura*, plain-coloured and short-finned, is recorded from the coast of Queensland but belongs properly to the South Sea islands where its range extends as far east as the Society Islands (longitude 144° W).

The common eel of Queensland rivers is the mottled *Anguilla reinhardti*, which attains a length of well over 1m. This species is also found in some islands to the east but is scarce south of Sydney.

Freshwater eels abound in the islands of the Indo-Pacific region but they are not uniformly distributed. They are absent from eastern Malaysia and from the eastern shores of many of the islands. To the west lies the deep water of the Indian Ocean while the waters to the east are shallow. The lack of suitable currents to carry the larvae from deep water elsewhere explains the situation.

The species found widely through the islands are *A. marmorata, A. celebesensis, A. bicolor* and, less commonly, *A. nebulosa, A. interioris* and *A. borneensis. A. ancestralis* has recently been declared non-existent by Castle and Williamson. It did not seem to be a convincing species as described by Ege, and in 1971 Dr Gordon Williamson hunted vigorously for it and other eels in northern Sulawesi (formerly Celebes). He found *A. marmorata, A. celebesensis, A. borneensis* and *A. bicolor*, but no trace of *A. ancestralis*. The first three were found only in rivers but *A. bicolor* was more widely distributed, in swamps and paddy-

Illus 10 World distribution of freshwater eels (shaded). Breeding ground of European eel marked **X**

fields. *A. marmorata* was the most abundant species.

Anguilla celebesensis is a mottled eel which reaches a length of $1\frac{1}{2}$m. *A. interioris* apparently is a rather small species, also mottled, reaching 70cm and is known only from New Guinea. *A. borneensis* is long-finned, plain coloured and small, about the same size as *A. interioris*. It has been found in Borneo and Sulawesi. *A. bicolor* and *A. nebulosa* have much more extensive ranges and are known from the rivers of India, Sri Lanka, southern Africa and Malagasy. The last two species can both be

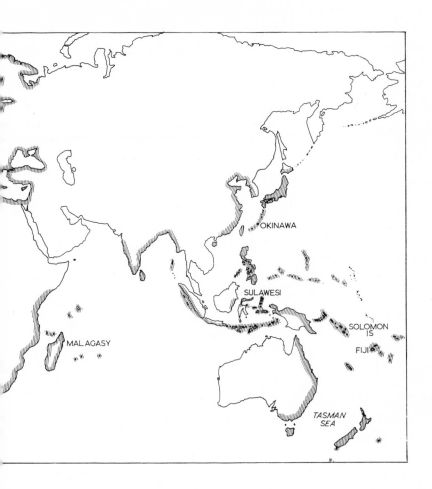

divided into separate races and apparently have several different spawning grounds. This would be expected when the immense distances between the populations are considered.

The eels of southern Africa have been described in some detail in a paper by R. A. Jubb of the Albany Museum, Grahamstown. He lists six species including strays of *A. anguilla* which has been recorded from Kenya, having presumably wandered through the Suez Canal, and *A. obscura* which was once found in the Buffalo river. *A. marmorata* is uncommon, the rivers of Malagasy are the true home of this species in the western Indian Ocean.

Elvers of the three common species, *A. nebulosa*, *A. bicolor* and *A. mossambica* reach the rivers of the east coast of Africa in January and February. *A. mossambica* elvers are found between latitudes 21° and 31° S but the other two stay north of 20°. However, older eels of *A. nebulosa* move southwards in the sea and subsequently enter rivers so that their range overlaps with *A. mossambica*. *A. nebulosa* is a mottled eel, *A. mossambica* is long-finned and plain coloured. These eels make extremely long journeys inland and along the coasts. *A. nebulosa* was collected by Winifred Frost at Chirundu Bridge, 1,000km from the sea, and the ranges of adult eels may be as much as 3,000km from the regions where the elvers are found. Males are more plentiful in rivers which enter the sea within the elver zones. Migration of the silver eels takes place from October to March when the summer rains give rise to floods which make the passage of the eels safer.

The African eels are supposed to breed in a region to the east of Malagasy between latitudes 10° and 20° S and longitudes 60° and 65° E. The South Equatorial Current flows westwards from this region, dividing into northwards and southwards streams where it meets Malagasy, after which it reaches the African coast.

In India and Sri Lanka only two species of eel are found: *A. bicolor* and *A. nebulosa*. *A. bicolor* is the smaller of the two, reaching a length of 60cm and keeping to coastal waters. *A. nebulosa* grows to over 1m and travels much farther inland. The Indian populations of these species may have separate spawning grounds from the African and Indo-Pacific races. Two sub-species of each are recognised but do not really help to explain the situation. The Indian race of *A. bicolor* is that found also in Africa, but the African race of *A. nebulosa* is not the same as the Indian.

Finally there are the eels of the South Sea islands, north and south of latitude 20° S: three species have been recorded from many localities. The range of *A. obscura* extends eastwards to Tahiti and this, with the South African record, give it and the next species the widest distribution of all freshwater eels. The range of *A. marmorata* extends eastwards to the Marquesas at longitude 139° and, with its occurrence in Japanese and South African waters, makes it the most widely distributed. Nearly as wide a range is shared by *A. obscura* which goes eastwards to Tahiti and west to South Africa, perhaps all coming from a single breeding area and therefore arguably the most travelled species. One species, *A. megastoma* is confined to the Pacific islands from the Solomons to Pitcairn at 130° E, and there the eastward records stop.

Details of the classification of freshwater eels and their distribution are given in the monumental paper by Wilhelm Ege, published by the Carlsberg Foundation and incorporating the results of the *Dana's* circumnavigation of 1928 to 1930. Even this great work leaves enormous gaps in our understanding of the group and there is scope for a great deal of work on both large and small scales. As already mentioned, one of the sixteen species of eels described by Ege has recently been dropped and it is possible that others may be declared invalid. While the study of body proportions, vertebral counts and colours has served to clarify the situation, both ecological observations and biochemical studies will help greatly in the future. Many of the sub-species may in fact merit specific rank.

Ege's treatise on eels is strictly for the specialist. An earlier paper by Schmidt published in 1925, 'On the Distribution of the Fresh-water Eels (*Anguilla*) Throughout the World', gives a much more readable account of the subject although it is naturally more tentative in its conclusions. This paper includes some very interesting material on traditional fisheries and on the eel in folklore in the Pacific islands.

The freshwater eels are classified on criteria of relative lengths of the dorsal and anal fins, colour and arrangement of the teeth. Attempts have been made to relate this classification to evolutionary development but the matter remains highly controversial.

There is little doubt, however, that the genus arose in what is now the Indo-Pacific region and descended from some ancestor which inhabited deep, warm oceanic water.

MIGRATION OF MARINE EELS

The migration of the marine eels has not been studied to the same degree as that of the freshwater species. There seems to be a tendency for all kinds to move away from coastal waters and to spawn over greater depths. Morays and snake eels may spawn in water as shallow as 100 or 200m. This can be found quite close to the haunts of the adults so no lengthy migrations are required. In deep ocean water both adults and larvae of thread eels and others may be seen together. In this case the deep water required for spawning is available where the adults live.

Some marine species, however, are known to have long larval lives and to make journeys of distances approaching those of the freshwater eels. The conger was one of the first to be traced and its life cycle in the Atlantic was described by Schmidt as early as 1912. Young larvae were found near the surface of water from 3,000–4,000m deep between Gibraltar and the Azores. This, however, is not the sole spawning place: young conger larvae are plentiful in the Mediterranean as well.

The eggs of the conger are laid at midsummer and the larval life lasts one or two years. A large female may produce 10 million eggs. Just as in the case of the freshwater eel, no spawning adults have ever been captured on or even near the spawning grounds. However, maturing individuals have been watched in aquaria where they stop feeding and gradually degenerate as eggs or sperm develop. The skin becomes darker and the eyes large. As calcium is drained from the skeleton, the bones become soft. Whether this degree of degeneration takes place under natural conditions is not known, but it is assumed that no congers survive to spawn a second time.

The breeding of *Enchelycore nigricans*, a fish-eating eel of the tropical Atlantic, involves migration in the opposite direction to that of the European freshwater eel. *Enchelycore* breeds off the coast of Africa near the Cape Verde Islands in May and June and migrates 3,000km southwards as far as the river Bony. Some of the population, however, travel across the Atlantic and are found in the Gulf of Mexico and on the coast of South America. Presumably they head back across the ocean when they reach maturity.

The remarkable habits of the freshwater eels therefore are simply an extension of a universal pattern for the order of eels. Spawning must take place in warm water of considerable depth. Some species live permanently close to or even within the breeding area. Others travel inshore and may enter lagoons and estuaries while the extreme cases, represented in several families of eels, are capable of living in fresh water. Wherever they feed and grow, however, it seems that all must return to some warm, deep ocean birthplace.

5

CATCHING EELS

It is possible to capture an eel by hand, scooping it out of the water as it feeds. The occasions when this can be done are rare, but eels are good to eat and other methods of capture have been devised in the course of thousands of years. The eel is uncommonly good at escaping from normal fishing gear but fishermen have shown equal skill in developing special techniques for capturing it. Some are simple and require a minimum of equipment, others are elaborate and costly, but the insatiable desire for eels has raised their value high enough to allow for considerable investment.

All fishing gear can be divided into two classes: active and passive. Active gear comprises equipment such as trawls and spears, used to pursue the fish to the point of capture. With passive gear, such as baited hooks and fixed nets, the fisherman's hunting ends with his finding promising places where he sets his apparatus to let the fish catch itself. In eel fishing there is another two-way division of methods, depending on whether the hunt is for sedentary eels or for migrating eels. In this chapter we consider first of all the gear for sedentary or yellow eels since this includes the most primitive methods and also presents the greatest variety.

FISHING WITH BAITED LINES

The most primitive passive gear is a bunch of earthworms and a piece of string. The technique, known as 'bobbing' or 'clotting', is most effective at night and is widely used by small-scale fishermen. The worms are threaded on a length of coarse string which may be attached to a pole. The bait is duly lowered into the water and a phase which may be extremely passive begins. As soon as a bite is felt the string is jerked out of the water. Professionals keep a plastic or metal bath beside them so that the captive can be swung into this rather than landed on the grass.

Opinion differs as to whether the eel is caught because it holds the worms with determination, or because its teeth get entangled in the threads of the string. Bobbing in fresh water has limited chances of success until near sunset or approaching dawn, when eels feed most actively. In muddy estuaries, where feeding takes place day and night, it may work well in daytime and, as a rule, piers and bridges are the favoured fishing positions.

These places are partly a matter of convenience for the fishermen. They may also be better than the open estuary since there are good hiding places for eels amongst the stonework. The fact that eels can so easily be attracted by worms is interesting. Earthworms do not form a normal part of the diet of freshwater eels, since as a rule they are not found in the water. However, at any time when floods break river banks and carry worms into the stream they are greedily taken by eels and indeed by other fish including trout. Earthworms are also one of the most effective baits for long-liners and anglers.

The eel gets short treatment in angling books. Perhaps its nocturnal habits are the greatest discouragement to sport fishermen. However, there is at least one book in English on the subject, by Raymond Perrett. Mr Perrett recommends a bait of earthworms for small eels, or small fish such as rudd for eels of more than 1kg. Tackle must be very strong because there is no possibility of wearing out an eel by playing it. If the eel once secures a hold of some solid object there is no hope of dislodging it.

A few jerks on the line indicates that the eel has taken the bait. It then moves off some distance, a big one for as much as 50m, and swallows the bait. This is the time to strike and the victim must be subjected to a relentless pull until brought to the landing net or bank. Since the fishing is probably taking place in the dark and the eel usually swallows bait and hook, recovery of the hook on the spot is not attempted. There is no point, either, in trying to grasp the eel. The angler holds the trace and lowers the captive into a sack. The mouth of the sack is shut and tied and the trace cut. Fishing continues with a new hook and trace. The British angling record eel was a specimen of 3.85kg (8½lb) caught near Bristol in 1922; but eels of at least 5kg (11lb) have been recorded.

Izaak Walton devotes most of his chapter on the eel to its habits and to long-lining but he does provide a useful paragraph on the art of 'snigling' :

And because you, that are but a young angler, know not what snigling is, I will now teach it to you. You remember, I told you, that eels do not usually stir in the day time; for then they hide themselves under some covert; or under boards or planks about flood gates or weirs or mills; or in holes on the river banks; so that you, observing your time in a warm day, when the water is lowest, may take a strong small hook, tied to a strong line, or to a string about a yard long; and then into one of these holes or between any boards about a mill or under any great stone or plank or any place where you think an eel may hide or shelter herself, you may, with the help of a short stick, put in your bait, but leisurely, and as far as you may conveniently; and it is scarce to be doubted, but if there be an eel, within the sight of it, the eel will bite instantly, and as certainly gorge it; and you need not doubt to have him if you pull him not out of the hole too quickly, but pull him out by degrees; for he, lying folded double in his hole, will, with the help of his tail, break all, unless you give him time to be wearied with pulling; and so get him out by degrees, not pulling too hard.

The paragraph is full of shrewd observations. In particular the recommendation to choose a warm day with low water. Warm, sunny weather encourages eels to abandon their usual nocturnal habits and seek food in the open.

Walton also stressed the need for stealth in bringing the bait near the eel and, when it has bitten, the need for patient pressure to bring it in. Eels can hold themselves very firmly in holes or crevices by exerting pressure with their tails on opposite sides. This ability is shared by congers and morays and in this lies their danger to divers.

Satisfying though the single line with a single hook may be, it will not yield enough eels in a day for a professional fisherman. By far the most popular method of bait-fishing therefore is the long-line, and it is widely used in lakes over most of the eel's habitat. In salt or brackish water it is less satisfactory because a large proportion of the bait is liable to be taken by crabs.

A long-line consists of a main line which may be up to 1 or 2km in length to which hooks on 'droppers' are attached at intervals, usually of 2m. The length of the dropper must not be more than half the distance between it and the next one on the main line. If the droppers are longer than this the adjacent hooks get tangled with one another. Small hooks tend to capture small eels, which are difficult to sell in many countries.

In Ireland long-lining used to be popular and many lakeside-dwelling fishermen worked at it in their own lakes in summer. More recently however its popularity has declined and, although a good number of fishermen still operate in Lough Neagh and Lough Erne, the other lakes are fished almost completely by three or four families who travel the country, bringing a boat with them and spending only a week or two in each lake.

Small whitefish are agreed to be the most effective bait in northern Europe. As with the earthworm, the attractiveness of this species is a little surprising since eels seldom have easy access to it under normal circumstances. It seems likely that some scent from the bait animal which has been injured in being impaled on the hook attracts the eel. The smell of fresh blood may be the important factor. A long-dead bait is totally ineffective.

The need for the bait to be fresh entails daily use of the long-line and daily baiting of every one of the thousand or so hooks. Under favourable conditions the capture of a thousand young whitefish is not too great a problem. In Ireland, Lough Neagh is the only lake which contains a large population of whitefish (known locally as pollan), and perch fry are widely used. Late in the season such small fish are unobtainable and earthworms must be sought. The daily capture of a thousand earthworms is not an easy task and becomes even more difficult in dry weather when the ground is hard and the worms burrow deeply.

To prepare for the night's fishing, the line is laid down neatly. A large wooden wheel may be used for the purpose, each hook being stuck into the rim. Otherwise a shallow wooden box serves. The line is coiled on the floor of the box while each hook is arranged in order (Plate 6). It is of course essential that no tangling should take place. Round about sunset the line is set.

Illus 11 Preparing a long-line – in the course of fishing the line has been heaped loosely in the box to the fisherman's left. He is engaged in checking the hooks, attaching new ones where necessary and arranging the line with the hooks in order in the box to his right. The hooks will be baited as the line is set

A lead sinker is attached to the leading end and, as the line is paid out, the hooks are baited.

About dawn the following morning the lines are lifted again. The captured eels apparently remain relatively quiet in the dark but become upset in the daylight when their struggles may tangle the line, or lead to their escape. The length of the dropper is again critical in this. If it is too long, tangling with its neighbour is possible; but if it is much shorter than the length of an eel it is more likely to tangle with the main line as the eel struggles to get free.

No attempt is made to remove the hook from the eel. Sometimes the victim is only loosely hooked through the jaw and drops off the line into the boat. Usually the bait and hook have been swallowed, and then the dropper is cut so that the eel falls into the holding box and the line can be folded into its container. The knife for cutting the dropper is fixed to the edge of the holding box and the dropper is severed by swinging it, with eel attached, against the blade.

SPEARING

Next to bare hands, spearing is one of the oldest ways of active fishing. Spears (Illus 2) have been used in all countries inhabited by eels and several different types have been developed. The greatest drawback of spearing is that it wounds the eels making them difficult to keep for long periods and lowering their value in a quality market. This does no harm to a man fishing for his supper, but counts for much when the catch is to be sold. Spear-fishing for eels is banned or strictly controlled in many countries. In Germany it is restricted to older fishermen who are unable to handle heavier gear. In Denmark it is forbidden in inland waters.

In Ireland Dr A. E. J. Went studied the distribution of eel spears and found that they were used formerly in all the principal eel fisheries. More recently, spearing became confined to one area of mud flats near Rosslare on the south-east coast. In the

1960s changes in water currents covered this mud with sand and eels and fishery disappeared.

The season was limited to January and February when eels were so scarce that a reasonable price was paid even for the speared product. The eels lay buried in the mud below low-tide mark and fishing took place at low water. The fishermen knelt in a flat-bottomed boat, a spear in each hand. Thrusting the spears into the mud served both to catch the eels and to propel the boat.

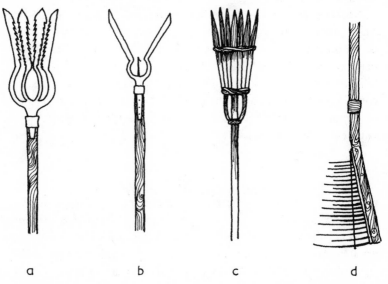

a   b   c   d

Illus 12 Eel spears: a, b European spears; c Maori spear; d European comb

Single-pronged spears may be used, but the usual eel spear has a pair of prongs or as many as four or five. Fig 6 shows a number of spears from various countries. The designs are universal, a case either of parallel evolution or of methods spreading with migrating people. A variant of the spear is the clamp. Here the jaws are replaced by spring clamps and less damage is caused to the eel. A modern development is the Danish eel tongs. The jaws are pulled together by a rubber band or spring activated by a trigger when the eel is touched.

Eel spearing by daylight is a hit-or-miss affair, thrusting the spear at random into mud where the eels live. The depth of the water can be anything from 1m or so down to 20m. The limiting factor is partly one of convenience – the shorter the spear the easier it is to handle so that thrusts may be made quickly and a greater area covered. The handle of the spear is usually wooden and its buoyancy therefore increases with the length. A length of 7m is considered to be about the limit, though with a weighted spear-head a handle of 20m has been used. This can scarcely be a convenient implement and it is difficult to see how the fisherman can tell he has caught a fish.

Eel may also be speared at night with the aid of a light and Professor von Brandt has described a curious fishery in Malagasy. There, small stone houses have been built over the outlets of lakes and migrating eels are caught in them by aimed spearing with the aid of a light. Apparently the light does not inhibit the movement of the eels.

One further development of the eel spear is the eel comb, used in Europe and Asia. The comb, fitted with many sharp straight prongs, is drawn through the mud and pierces any eels that lie in its path. This is not too efficient and many wounded eels escape. In Japan a 2-pronged eel comb is used to catch swimming eels at night with the aid of a light.

CAGE TRAPS FOR YELLOW EELS

The burrowing habits of eels have led to the development of a variety of cage traps. The cheapest and simplest are rigid and portable and are usually set in series, anchored to ropes. At the other extreme are enormous net barriers, fixed to stakes. From the small trap to the net barrier there is a continuous succession of traps, growing in complexity.

Three distinct principles are used in the design of traps. The first is to prepare a shelter for the eel to lie in in daytime. The second is to entice it into the trap with a bait. The third is to place in its path a barrier which leads to a cage.

The simplest trap of all has been devised by the resourceful eel fishermen of Malagasy. They dig small holes underwater which the eels enter, presumably in preference to burrowing for themselves. The fishermen dive down and spear the eels. A development from this is used in Japan. Instead of digging holes, a bundle of three bamboo tubes is placed in the water. The smallest trap of this kind has a bore of 2cm diameter and a length of 70cm – considerably longer than the biggest eel that could enter it. These traps have no valves and must be lifted carefully so that the eels stay inside.

I developed the same device quite independently for use in my studies of an eel in an aquarium. A piece of black PVC pipe of 25mm bore and about 40cm long lying on the bottom of the tank provided the eel with a shelter from the daylight. When I wanted to take her out for monthly weighing and measuring sessions, I simply placed my hands over each end and lifted eel and pipe from the water. Her desire to keep hidden when frightened meant that she made no attempt to leave the tube when I brought my hands close to it.

The next step is a trap with a valve. The opening of the trap is conical, the wide mouth providing an easily found entrance which leads to the narrow inner opening at the apex of the cone. When this sort of valve is used for capturing lobsters or birds it needs no modification : the victims have very little chance of rediscovering the inner opening and, even if they succeed, it is difficult for them to make their way through it. But the eel is not so easily fooled and the trap must be developed further.

A universal eel trap is shaped like a barrel or bottle with a funnel entrance at one end and a hinged cover at the other. A typical design was used until recently in the estuary of the river Suir in the south of Ireland (Illus 13). Woven from willow stems, it is bottle-shaped with the entrance at the wide end. The funnel extends nearly the full length of the trap. Instead

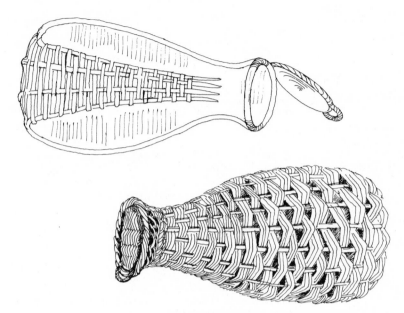

Illus 13 Wicker eel pot, Carrick-on-Shannon, Ireland

of being neatly bent over to form a ring at the inner end, the warp stems of the funnel are left sticking out and are even sharpened to make a ring of spikes. Presumably these hurt the eels when they try to find the way out and encourage them to retire to a comfortable position at the wide end. The narrow end of the trap is closed by a hinged door which can be opened to insert bait and to remove the catch. These traps are baited with fresh 'sprat' – in fact a variety of small fishes – and are tended at least once, and preferably twice, a day. The attractiveness of the bait falls off quickly as the fishes lose their fresh smell so it is unlikely that any eels enter the trap after a few hours. If the trap is left too long without attention some of the eels manage to escape. Chicken or rabbit offal are often recommended as bait but they would need to be very fresh.

Traps of this kind are used all over the world. There are many local variations both in materials used and in shape, though the dimensions are fairly constant. The trap is about 1m

103

in length with a diameter of 30–50cm. The size is a compromise between the smallest which will admit a good-sized eel and the biggest that can be handled conveniently from a small boat. Alternative materials include wooden laths or PVC rods tied together with plastic-coated wire. The distance between the laths varies between 2 and 8mm depending on the size of eel to be caught. The 8mm gap is adequate for well-grown eels, the narrow gap entails a heavier and more expensive trap but is essential if small eels are needed. The traps can be made more effective if a hose of fine-meshed netting is attached to the inner opening of the funnel. It should hang fairly loosely, but may be pulled out by a string attached to the body of the trap opposite the opening. Such a net can easily be opened by the eel swimming into the trap, but hides the entrance to the funnel as soon as the victim has passed it. A nylon stocking in this position is effective.

Traps of wicker or lath were popular enough when labour was cheap. They can still be considered where time is on the side of the fisherman and is not being reckoned in terms of wages per hour. In affluent countries such hand-made gear no longer pays. Moulded plastic has made an entry here and, on account of the high cost of preparing the mouldings, a single design is widely used in western Europe. The arrival of this trap in a new area invariably leads to comments on moon rocketry. The only variation is a choice between a short trap with one funnel and a long trap with two. The entrance is a wide-mouthed funnel with an oval cross-section. The body of the trap is nearly cylindrical with an inner funnel attached at the mouth. In the short trap the other end of the cylinder leads into a conical cap with a hinged lid. In the long trap it leads to a second cylinder and funnel which in turn goes to the nose cone. A pair of iron rods attached to each cylinder weigh the trap down and the upper side is a solid sheet, providing the eels with shelter from the light. The inner end of the second funnel is further reduced by a crown of fine, pliable strips of the plastic, longer than the diameter of the opening and pointing towards the cap. These

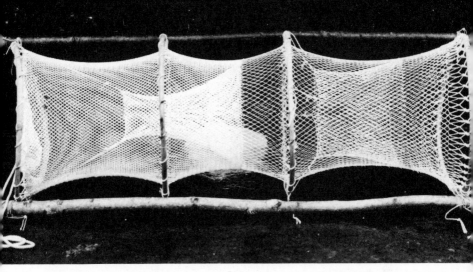

Illus 14 A collapsible eel-pot, or basket, attached to two poles for fishing. Notice the large mesh and four-sided funnel of the 'parlour', smaller mesh and slit-opening of the inner end

can easily be brushed aside by the eel entering the trap, but close the gap when it tries to return. This restricted opening, if placed in the outer funnel, might scare the eel and prevent it from trying to go in. Once the victim has passed the first funnel the crown opening is the easiest way of escape and so it pushes past it. So the short trap is cheaper and easier to handle, but needs more frequent attention since the eel may find the way out rather easily.

These traps are usually baited and set in rivers or estuaries, many being attached in rows to a single rope. The baskets are normally used with bait and need the current to spread the scent of the bait over a wide area, attracting the eels. I have seen the plastic traps set in a river for a week or more and there, if any bait had been used, it would have ceased to be effective. It seems that the eels were entering these traps in search of shelter rather than for food, the principle here being the same as in the Japanese bamboo traps. Possibly such traps may be effective in some lakes but they are generally regarded as river-gear and my own experience in trying them in lakes has been consistent and dismal failure.

The eel basket has developed recently in two directions. One is towards traps of wire or fibre netting. The general design can easily be copied using galvanised wire mesh on wire hoops. The netting essentially is the same as the trap used in the summer fyke net (page 108). It is transformed into a basket type simply by attaching the hoops to a pair of wooden rods as shown in Illus 14. These traps are normally used with bait and in Ireland they have replaced the wicker traps in the river Suir estuary. In this case the new design was introduced by a visiting Dutch fisherman who brought the traps with him. Their efficiency impressed the local fishermen so much that they adopted the idea without delay. Their only drawback was the ever-present irritation of the invasion of the traps by innumerable shore crabs.

The other development of the trap is towards a wooden box. Naturally it is easier and much cheaper to build a simple box than to weave laths or willow wands. In the Dutch IJsselmeer fishery, eel boxes were developed a few years ago and proved effective and simple to use. The boxes were described by Dr C. L. Deelder at the EIFAC Consultation in 1970.

The trap is a narrow box (Illus 15), 70cm long and with a height and width of about 11cm. (Because of the very intensive fishery in the IJsselmeer, eels of more than 70cm are virtually unknown and most of the captives are much smaller.) The box is made from wooden battens 1cm thick, nailed together, and has a sliding lid on the upper side. On the lower side two iron bars are fitted to weigh the trap down on the bottom and keep

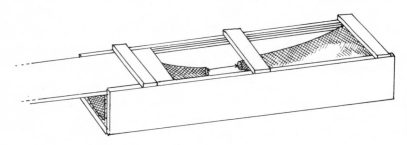

Illus 15   Dutch eel box

it horizontal. The ends of the box are left open so that it forms a rectangular tube, and the openings form frames for a pair of nylon-mesh funnels. These funnels are kept stretched by a piece of string connecting their ends together.

Each box is attached to a long rope by a piece of cord of about 1m. They are placed at intervals of 25m apart on the rope, each end of which may be marked with a buoy. In places where fish-stealing is too regular, traps such as these, and long-lines too, are set without buoys, and the hauling-line is picked up by searching with a grappling hook. The number of boxes used depends on the size of the boat and the crew. In the IJsselmeer a crew of 3 can handle 300 which entails a hauling rope of about 7km in length.

Each box must be baited daily. Smelt is the most popular bait-fish in Holland. Smelt are small estuarine fish, 10 or 15cm long. Their effectiveness as a bait almost certainly depends on the fact that they have a particularly strong smell, rather like cucumbers, which attracts the eels from a considerable distance.

The sensitivity of eels to smells is very clearly shown by the use of these traps. New boxes are useless. They must be kept in the water for several weeks to develop the proper smell. Apparently they even take some time to attain the smell of a particular water, so that they cannot be moved indiscriminately from lake to lake. Some plywoods proved successful in experiments, others did not on account of the different types of wood used. The success of the boxes was shown dramatically by the catch figures over their first five years of operation, from nothing in 1965 to nearly 500 tons in 1970. It is interesting that such a simple trap apparently was not introduced to European fisheries until a few years ago. Possibly the fact that it took so long for the eels to accept a trap made of new wood discouraged experimenters. If wooden boxes had been tried in the past they might have been discarded as useless when they failed to catch eels in the first week or so. Pressure to persist in experiments of this kind came from the increasing unsuitability of the long-line on account of its high labour-content.

The traps so far described depend on attracting the eels either to a sheltered place or to food. On lake bottoms there is mud or dense vegetation to burrow in. The weakness of the water currents reduces the dispersal of the smell of a bait and so there is little to induce eels to enter such traps. Conceivably there are local conditions where they might work but, as already mentioned, I have tried traps in many lakes and have been disappointed.

Fishing gear to be used in lakes must therefore depend on some other phase of eel activity. The principle used is to place an obstruction in the way of eels as they wander in search of food and to guide them into traps.

Eels must swim hither and thither on the lake bottom to hunt for invertebrates. Fish such as trout usually stay in one place and wait for invertebrates to swim past them. Pike and similar predators lurk and pounce out on unsuspecting fish. Possibly some eels do this too, but the majority appear to wander.

If a wandering eel meets a wall of netting on the bottom it makes no serious attempt to swim through or over it but changes its direction and swims along it for a few metres. I do not know how or when this fact was discovered, but it gave rise to the development of a simple and very effective trap, the fyke net. The fyke consists essentially of a wall of net called the leader to guide the eel into a trap fixed at the end.

The trap is made of nylon mesh, supported by circular hoops. The hoops may be made of cane, stainless steel or plastic tubing. In my experience cane was rather bulky and heavy. Plastic tubing, although light, was rather weak and liable to damage when used in difficult conditions. Stainless steel was the most satisfactory and outlasted the netting material, even in salt water. The choice, however, was limited, since each netting factory seldom prepared a cheap, production-line net of more than one kind.

The design of a typical trap is similar to the eel pot shown in Illus 14, but it is kept open by being anchored at each end or by being used as a member of a long train of nets, anchored at the ends. The trap shown has two funnels, the first is attached to the first hoop of the trap and leads to a wide, rectangular inner opening, supported by four strings attached to the third hoop. This first inner opening is wide so that the eel will swim fairly passively into the 'parlour' or front part of the trap. Her suspicions must not be aroused at this stage. If they are, she will simply turn back and swim away. The mesh at the outer end is 16mm and at the cod-end 12mm. The latter mesh size allows eels of less than about 35cm to escape. In the Mediterranean coastal lagoons, where there is a sale for very small eels, smaller cod-end meshes may be used.

The second funnel is attached to the wall of the net between the third and fourth hoops. Its inner opening is supported by only two strings, so that it forms a vertical slit, easily pushed open by the eel but very difficult for her to find once she has passed it. No doubt this narrow opening does scare the eel. But if she turns back at this stage she will probably find her way only to the blind end of the parlour and then return to the slit as the lesser of two evils. The toe or cod-end of the trap is kept closed by a purse-string so that it can be opened easily by the fisherman. Longer traps with three funnels are sometimes preferred.

The size of the trap is very variable and it is difficult to know whether the variations have been dictated by logic or whether they depend on the whim of individual fishermen who happened to like particular designs. The first small fyke that I saw in use was a Dutch one. Its opening hoop was D-shaped, with the diameter arranged to lie on the ground, supposedly to prevent eels from swimming underneath it. It was about 1m in height and the whole trap was 4 or 5m long. It happened to be the smallest that would fit in my car and I got a supply for my experiments. They worked well.

A year or two later a Danish fisherman came to Ireland to

fish with a much smaller kind of net, about 50cm in height and perhaps 3m long. These were so much more convenient than my Dutch ones that I set to work with them. They, too, worked well. The makers stopped supplying these nets after a while and the next batch, from a different factory, were smaller. The same happened once more, and the last factory came up with something smaller still. I compared my results and came to the conclusion that the smallest traps, cheapest and most convenient, were every bit as good as the biggest. It is, of course, extremely difficult to make really sound comparative trials of fishing gear for eels. The behaviour of the quarry depends so much on weather, water currents and the precise position of the net that it is always difficult to be sure of precisely what causes a difference in the catch.

One very plausible suggestion made by Professor von Brandt is that the distance between the inner opening of the first funnel and the constriction of the second must be greater than the length of the eel to be caught. The idea is that, if the victim's suspicions are aroused by the second funnel before her tail has left the first, she will be able to escape backwards. There is probably some truth in this and it does seem wise to allow a distance of 50cm or so between these two positions. But this was the distance in my smallest traps, and these caught many eels of 70cm and more. Clearly the exact measurement is not so very important – theoretically my traps should not have caught 70cm eels or even any bigger than 50cm.

The only reason I can see for a large trap is to make room for a large catch of eels. A small fyke trap can hold 10 to 20kg of eel. Under normal Irish conditions I counted myself lucky to catch even 1kg per trap, but there were exceptions. The most interesting fact was that the presence of other trapped eels apparently made no difference to the numbers that would try to enter. Where the eel population was really dense, many of the traps after a night's fishing would come up packed tight with eels, each one having squeezed its way in to join the first captives.

This desire for company has been seen amongst eels in aquarium tanks as well as in the wild, but it appears to be a reaction to stress. H. Mohr described how newly caught eels sought each others' company in a tank. They would gather together in a mass or all try to force themselves into the same tube. Under these conditions they did not bite each other nor did the large individuals try to bully the small ones. After four weeks of life in the tank, however, the eels would go back to their normal individualistic habits. None would tolerate another in its tube and the small ones were driven out of their shelters and bitten.

However small may be the effect of the size of the trap part of the fyke net, the dimensions and shape of the guiding wall of netting are quite another matter. As in the parlour of the trap, the mesh size in the guide wall or 'leader' can be fairly large, 16 or 18mm, since the eel will not try very hard to swim through it. The leader is the same height as the diameter of the first hoop of the trap, or a little higher. Its lower edge is held down by a leaded sole rope and the upper edge is fitted with buoys at intervals. These are buoyant enough to make the net stand up as a wall, but not so light that they raise the lead-line off the bottom.

It would be logical to think that the lead-line should be very firmly weighted down so that no gap appears between the lower edge of the leader and the ground. On the assumption that the eel is swimming on the very bottom, it might be expected to find any gap between net and ground and swim out through it. I have been pleasantly surprised at how well the nets have worked on very rough rocky ground or where weed growth held the leader up in places. Such 'bad' settings gave satisfactory results.

The simplest arrangement of fyke nets dispenses altogether with the leader and this arrangement is used sometimes in rivers. A train of traps, the mouth of each fixed by two strings to the toe of the next, are anchored firmly at the upstream end. It is difficult to know just how they attract eels, but they are quite effective.

The next stage is a trap with a single leader. This kind and the next are usually attached to stakes driven into the mud but as an alternative they may be anchored to submerged heavy weights, especially in places where fish-stealing is a way of life. A very common plan (Illus 16a) has a single leader fixed at right angles to the bank of a canal or lake and running to the first hoop of the trap. Usually such a leader is sewn into the funnel of the trap for a short distance, although it seems to work effectively if it is merely tied to top and bottom of the hoop.

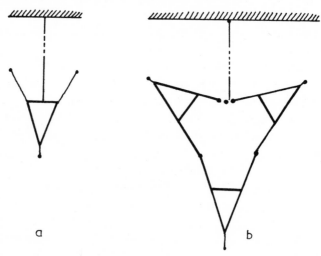

Illus 16   Fyke net arrangements

The mouth of the trap is often extended towards the leader on each side as a pair of 'wings'. A development of this uses three traps, one at the end of the leader and two at an angle to the first (Illus 16b). The subsidiary traps catch far fewer eels than the main one. This system is very popular in the French lagoons.

A variation of this trap dispenses with the central leader, replacing it with a pair of long wings. This kind is set in particular positions, such as where a canal or slow stream enters or leaves a lake and there is reason to believe that eels will be

Illus 17   Summer fyke-net train

moving in one direction. Many and greater developments of this plan of net are used for the capture of silver eels, to be considered later.

One of the simplest and most successful of fyke nets for yellow eels has been the 'summer fyke' or 'couple'. One unit of this consists of a pair of traps joined mouth to mouth by the leader (Illus 17). Summer fykes are set in long strings, attached end to end and paid out from a boat. A train of the nets can be operated single-handed but it is much easier for two fishermen to do the work. One rows the boat while the other pays out the net. In single-handed operation, hoops and meshes have an impressive facility for getting caught in anything that sticks out from the edge of the boat, even a small wooden splinter can upset the flow. One improvement I made was to pack each train of eight or ten nets in a polythene fertiliser sack. On a large commercial scale, however, as many as a thousand summer fykes may be used by a single boat.

The length of the leader of these nets is very important. Naturally 1m of leader costs very much less than 1m of trap. The principle in fishing is to cover as great a distance as possible in one setting operation so the economics require that the leader should be as long as possible in relation to the trap. However, there must be a limit to the distance an eel will swim along the leader before she decides to move away from it.

In the course of my experiments I used leaders of four different lengths: 9, 6.5, 4.7 and 3.3m. Sometimes it was possible to make up a train of nets of leaders of alternating lengths so that there was a fair chance of making a direct comparison of their efficiency. The longest leader, 9m, turned out to be the least effective. Presumably, any eels which met it anywhere near

113

its centre-point gave up following the line before they reached the traps. The second leader proved the best at 6.5m, and the shortest two caught slightly fewer eels than this. There was one exception to the rule. When eels were very sparse, either because the population was low in the area or because I was fishing too early in the season when the water was cold, the longest leader proved the most effective. However, under such conditions it was likely that eel fishing would not pay anyway so the 6.5m leader would seem to be the best.

A little qualification is necessary here. My experiments were made in Ireland mainly at temperatures between 13° and 18°C and I would expect that the results would apply to other countries with temperatures of this order. In lakes or rivers where the temperature in summer is higher or lower a different degree of activity might be expected, and the eels might settle for leaders of different lengths.

Summer fykes are easy to use in shallow lake-water, down to 3 or 4m. The train is fixed by 2 or 3m of light rope to a weight at each end. The weight which I use is made simply of a 1lb ($\frac{1}{2}$kg) food-can filled with cement. A wire loop is placed in the cement to make an attachment for the rope. In friendly neighbourhoods the ends of the net can be marked by a buoy. Elsewhere it is an easy matter to hide the net and pick it up with a grappling hook. A French fisherman assured me that this system would be useless in the lagoons where he operated, but did not explain why. He uses leaders which extend from surface to bottom.

A firmer anchoring device is needed where the nets are used in rivers or where there are strong tidal currents. In such cases a boat anchor, weighing about 1kg, is satisfactory. Although there is some tendency for the nets to roll about and for the leaders to get twisted in tidal water, the nets still work well. The inner funnels do, however, get blocked by drifting weed after a while so that there is no advantage in leaving the nets in a fishing position for more than a single tide interval. In my experience few or no eels are ever found on tidal mud and the nets must be set at low water to ensure that they are always below the surface. In estuaries the most irritating hazard of all is the fact that the fykes catch shore crabs with even greater efficiency than they catch eels. Shore crabs are seldom acceptable to fish buyers and they have impressive skill in entangling the nets.

The differing habits of eels in lakes, rivers and estuaries have already been mentioned in Chapter 3. They are so important in practical fishing that they are worth repeating here. The wanderings of eels in lakes appear to be very limited in the course of a summer, and there is little to be gained by leaving the nets in one position for more than a night. No harm will be done, however, if it is more convenient to leave them set for longer periods, from weekend to weekend for example. But a 7-day catch will certainly not contain seven times as many eels as the results of one day. In estuaries there is a much greater degree of local movement and a favoured position may yield good catches night after night. In the only extensive experiments I have made in a river I found that most of the large eels were caught on the first night, much smaller specimens turning up in the same place on successive fishing days.

Active gear other than spears has long been used for yellow-eel fishing. Seine nets, trawl nets and electrical gear are all used. The netting depends very much on a great area of lake bed free from obstructions being available, so that the net can be hauled without damage. Both forms of netting are frowned on by many eel experts on the grounds that the dragging of the net destroys the fauna and flora of the lake bed and seriously reduces the available food for eels and other fish. It has also been shown that trawling frightens the eels. It may take the survivors some weeks to recover from the experience and their lying in hiding over this period would reduce their rate of feeding and hence their growth. Trawling is therefore forbidden by law in many countries. That is not to say that it does not take place. Legal trawling and seining can, however, be seen in Western Germany where master fishermen lease exclusive rights to lake fisheries from the State. Where one man has such a right there are no competing fishermen to claim interference with his sport or livelihood. The situation is very different in countries where large fisheries are shared by all the citizens.

Eel seining in Germany has been described by M. Kaulin. The seine net consists of a bag with two long wings on each side (Illus 18). The wing length may be as much as 1,000m. The longer the net the more eels may be caught at a single haul but the limiting factors are the cost of so much netting and the manpower needed to operate a large net. Kaulin described as a typical example a medium-sized seine which is operated by a crew of five in three boats.

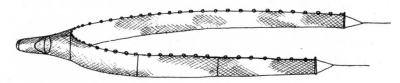

Illus 18   German eel seine

Each of the wings consists of 3 rectangular pieces of netting 65m in length when stretched. The first piece is about 6m deep, the second 7m and the third 8m, the depth increasing towards the bag. Each of the wings is 108m in length after mounting, and the depth of the net at the bag is about 12.5m. The fore-ends of the net are kept apart by a 1m stick and the bag is fitted with a funnel about half-way down to prevent the eels from swimming out.

Each wing of the net is stowed in one of the boats, the third boat is used at the end of the operation to pick up the bag. The two net-boats go together to the beginning of the operation. The bag is lowered first and then the net-boats make off in opposite directions either in a straight line or in a semi-circle, paying out the net as they go. After the wings have been set, the boats approach each other again and drop anchor some distance from the hauling place, paying out the hauling rope as they go. Each then winds in its rope using power winches.

In former times this was done by hand and larger and stronger crews were needed.

As soon as the rope is hauled and the spreader sticks of the net are aboard, the boats move to the hauling ground and drop anchor again. The hauling rope is attached to the anchor rope and the net is fixed to the stem of the boat. Each boat then winds in the hauling rope again so that boat and net are drawn towards the anchor. The final part of the hauling is done by hand. The wings must be taken on board carefully so that the ground rope is not lifted off the bottom, and usually the fishermen beat the water with sticks to frighten the eels back into the net. Finally the bag is taken aboard the third boat which has a box in which the eels can be kept alive.

Eel trawling has been practised in the Netherlands since 1500. Only fifty-five years later it went out of favour and was banned in inland waters as early as 1600. When the Zuider Zee was enclosed in 1932 trawling for eels was permitted, but it was again found to be a very damaging method. The production of eels was of the order of 10kg per ha where trawling was permitted, and about double this where other methods were used. Trawling was finally forbidden in the IJsselmeer, as the former Zuider Zee is called, in 1970.

Without doubt trawling is the most efficient means of catching eels in suitable regions. The question which will take longer to answer is whether occasional trawling yields a larger and more consistent catch in the long term. The Dutch experience suggests strongly that it does not and that less intensive methods are more profitable.

Since boats on inland waters where eel fishing takes place are usually small, otter trawling which needs powerful motors is seldom favoured. In Germany recent development has been towards pair trawling. The efforts of two boats are combined, both to keep the net wide open and to increase the dragging power. A detailed description of a specially designed eel trawl has been given by Dr R. Steinberg. The net is arranged to give the widest possible opening which entails having a low mouth :

apparently the eels make no attempt to swim up over the net so that a high opening is unnecessary. The bridle ropes are 12m in length and the length of the towing warp depends on the depth of the water : 40m of warp are enough for trawling in 2–3m of water while 120m are needed for a depth of 20m.

Two fishermen can operate the net between them. The trawl is first shot from one boat and the second then picks up the bridle at one side. Both boats now pay out enough warp line and sail parallel about half the length of the warp apart. In hauling the net the boats stop, and can be drawn back towards the net as the lines are winched in. Finally the bridle is detached from one boat and the net is hauled into the other. The net is fitted with a funnel in the cod-end.

The best catches are made at night and from 300 to 500 eels can be caught in a night's fishing, along with other fish like perch, roach and pike-perch. One very interesting result of the German experiments was that trawling was successful in April, long before trapping or line-fishing is effective.

The application of electricity to eel fishing has been studied in a number of countries. The ideal is to produce a current which induces the eels to swim straight into a net. This depends on the easily obtained experimental results of passing a direct current of suitable strength to induce the eels (or any other fish) to swim towards the anode. Too weak a current simply causes the victims to align themselves with the current, but not to swim to any great extent. Too strong a current produces 'galvano-narcosis', in other words stuns the fish as long as the current is switched on. The latter may cause severe damage or death.

Under field conditions the laboratory effects are not so easy to repeat. There are so many variables – electrical conductivity of the water, size of eel, temperature of the water and possibly a few as yet unknown – that the electrical eel-catcher seems to need a good deal more development. One authority suggests that a pulsed direct current of 30 to 50Hz is best for eels. Having seen eels caught by a fisherman's own invention which simply used a large number of lead-acid batteries in series and produced a steady current, I cannot help doubting this theory. When a pulsed current is used it seems that the shape of the wave is vital. A 'square' wave is much more effective than the more normal sine wave.

In streams, their maximum size generally defined by whether a fisherman can work them in thigh waders, portable electrical fishing machines catch eels effectively. These may be either powered by a 12V battery which drives a generator to produce a pulsed current of the order of 300V or by a heavier petrol-driven generator with direct or alternating current output. One electrode, a metal plate or rod, is fixed in the stream. The second (anode when direct current is used) forms the metal rim of a fine-meshed net. Eels of all sizes are narcotised close to the net and may be caught quite easily. In larger, swifter streams many individuals are frightened out of the electric field as the net approaches them, and escape.

Considerable success has been achieved in Germany and Poland in using electric current in conjunction with seine or trawl nets. It seems that a large proportion of the eels which have been concentrated by a normal trawl-net, escape in the final stages of hauling. Electrodes can be placed at the mouth of the net or between the wings some distance in front of it. Passage of a current of the order of 100–150V and 20–30amp apparently discourages them from trying to escape. To avoid damage to the fish the latter must be allowed to concentrate some distance from the electric field and it is recommended that the end of the bag be at least 10m from the field. The development of these nets has been described by Dr E. Halsband of Hamburg and Dr W. Dembinski and Dr A. Chmielewski of Poland. Incidentally, electrical fishing is as dangerous to fishermen as it is to fish. Dembinski and Chmielewski in their paper describe a highly desirable arrangement of safety devices.

SILVER EELS

Electrical fishing ends the section on hunting for yellow eels.

The next problem is to capture the mature, silver eels in the course of their downstream migration. The fact that they have ceased feeding means that there is no possibility of fishing with bait. The problem is simplified, however, by the habit of the silver eel to migrate in one direction and frequently in very large numbers. The principle therefore is one of designing barriers to the passage of the fish.

It is relatively easy to place in a river a barrier which will collect twigs and leaves, or even one which will prevent the passage of drowned animals or fallen tree trunks. Such a barrier must be strong enough to retain the objects it is designed to catch. It must also be able to be cleared easily so that an accumulation of leaves or such debris does not form a dam. There may be difficulties in the engineering aspects of the work, the greatest being to fix an immovable barrier in a river which may from time to time become a raging torrent. But the problem is relatively simple since the direction the debris will take is predictable, provided some details of the water currents are known.

Silver-eel fishing would be equally simple if the matter were merely one of filtering inanimate objects from the flood. But silver eels, although often pictured as being involved in a headlong rush to the sea, are highly sensitive individual animals. As more and more effort is put into the study of eel behaviour it will become possible to design more efficient eel traps but, in the present state of our knowledge, silver-eel fishing is largely a matter of trial and error. Each fishery must be worked on its own merits and local experiments must be made. Having said that, however, the general principle remains that silver-eel fishing in rivers is largely a matter of filtering the eels from the water. In lakes it is more one of guiding the victims away from their chosen path into a trap.

Without doubt the most efficient form of silver-eel trap is a grid which completely screens a river. Such grids are frequently placed at waterfalls, or at watermill dams. The grid is usually horizontal, or slopes slightly upwards in the direction of the flow. It is made of wooden laths or steel rods running parallel to the stream and with gaps of 12mm between them. The thickness of the laths or rods will depend on the current and the width of the river. The wider the rods the cheaper the construction, but the greater the damming effect of the screen. The sloping screen is firmly fixed to the bed of the river or wall of the waterfall at its upstream end – eels will very easily find any gap large enough to get through. The downstream end is fitted with a vertical screen and on meeting this the eels, now out of the water, wriggle along it to one side where the only opening leads into a trap with a funnel entrance or to a well where the water level is too low to allow them to climb back to the screen. The water in this trap must be thoroughly aerated. There have been cases of the loss of the 'catch of the season' because the eels became overcrowded in the trap and suffocated.

It is difficult to see how such a trap could fail to catch all the silver eels leaving a river or lake and there may very well be cases where a complete catch is made. But eels have their own ways which do not necessarily correspond to the desires of the fisherman. In the south-east of Ireland there is a region of reclaimed land, the South Sloblands of Wexford, which includes a central lake. The only outlet from this lake is through a canal and a pump. Upstream of the pump in the canal lies a screen which cannot be passed by eels and which leads into an appropriate trap. In some years this trap catches many eels; in others it fails. Perhaps the explanation is that eels have highly irregular migrating habits, but some were once seen on a wet night wriggling across a roadway. They must have made their way up a metre or more of canal bank and no doubt subsequently made their way over a sea wall. The unanswerable question was : what had scared these individuals away from a screen and a trap which thousands of their fellows had entered in the past and would enter again?

The rigid screen arrangement is limited to relatively small rivers, and in larger waters silver eels are invariably caught in large conical nets called 'stow nets' or coghills. Shape and size of the nets varies according to local conditions. A net used on

Illus 19 A net fishery at a bridge on the Corrib in Galway. The nets are raised in the daytime to allow salmon to pass safely. The cod-ends of the nets can be seen draped over the railings of the gangway. When fishing, the eels are released into the corrugated iron chutes which lead to the holding boxes. Holding boxes need to be strong – notice the flood damage to the one on the right

the river Shannon at Killaloe measures 10m in length and has a rectangular mouth 2.3m wide and 3.36m deep. The mesh size in the first 2.5m of the net is 50mm, in the next 3.5m it is 16mm and in the cod-end 11mm. There is a funnel of 16mm mesh· attached between the 50mm and 16mm mesh sections and leading to near the 11mm section.

The vertical sides of the net-opening are attached by metal rings to a pair of stakes fixed in the river bed. The lower side is stretched between them so that it makes as firm a contact as possible with a concrete sill on the bed. The upper side of the net extends a little way above the surface. The force of the current keeps the net open in the fishing position. When the net is to be emptied the mouth is raised clear of the water by two poles which are attached to the lower corners. The cod-end, whose position is marked by a buoy, is picked up by a boat in which the eels are placed. When eels are migrating in large numbers the nets have to be emptied very frequently, perhaps every half-hour through the night. At slack times the nets are left in the fishing position overnight and emptied in the morning.

At Killaloe the fishing gear consists of a barrage of these nets spanning the river. They do not screen the river completely because a navigation channel has to be left open. Similar barrages are used in other fisheries, sometimes with a modification so that they can be fished without the use of a boat. In this case a bridge is built downstream of the mouths of the nets from which the cod-ends can be raised by ropes (Illus 19). In the Lough Neagh fisheries there is an arrangement of gates which can be operated so that the mouths of the nets being fished are closed off.

All these netting systems catch many eels and the fisheries are very profitable. They are also very inefficient. The Lough Neagh nets at Toomebridge are probably as soundly designed as may be and they are operated by fishermen of great experience. Nonetheless, at Coleraine on the river Bann, 35km downstream from Toomebridge, there is a second series of nets and these too make excellent catches. The great majority of the eels taken by the Coleraine nets are individuals which have escaped through the Toomebridge barrage. Similarly, an experimental net placed downstream of the Killaloe fishery proved so successful that it has been maintained as a very important supplement to the catch. Although the Killaloe nets form a barrage across about nine-tenths of the width of the river, it is reckoned that they catch only between 16 and 40 per cent of the migrating eels. Tagging experiments which I made in various parts of Ireland also indicated that all the eel traps investigated allowed large proportions of the eels to escape. The most likely explanation of the failure of these traps is that the eels, highly

123

sensitive to pressure changes, are upset by the impedance of the current by the nets and make considerable efforts to find a clear passage downstream.

Fixing the row of stakes or posts needed to hold a barrage of stow nets is not always possible. Sometimes the size and strength of the river is so great that the cost of the engineering work cannot be justified. Often fishermen wish to operate in navigable rivers and cannot mount a permanent structure which would interfere with the shipping. Since river transport frequently stops at night it is possible to fish for eels, provided the gear can be held on some movable structure. Two ingenious solutions to this problem have been developed.

In one case the main support for the nets is an anchored boat. The nets, as many as four to a boat, are each kept open at the mouth by a rectangular iron frame. The frames are hung from beams held in position by rope and pulley tackle from the mast of the boat. They can be raised clear of the water by a winch. The frames are kept standing upright in the current by a bridle system which is attached to the boat anchor (Illus 20). Details

Illus 20 In German rivers, a boat at anchor is used where local conditions prevent the erection of a permanent structure for the support of eel nets. Here may be seen a boat-operated stow net

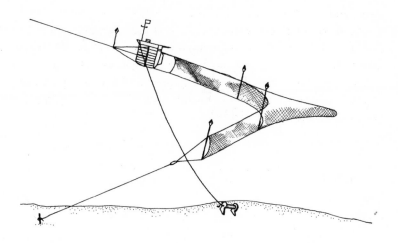

Illus 21   Otter-board stow net, river Elbe

of this method and the next are given in a paper by G. Klust.

The second system, developed by H. Koethke of Gorleben on the river Elbe, uses an otter-board to draw the net out across the river. The net used has relatively long wings and a single stow is used at each of several favoured positions on the river. The wings measure 20–25m in length. One wing is attached to the bank. The other is fixed to a large otter-board made of wood and iron, measuring 4m long by 3m high. It is suspended from the surface by a cylindrical float the same length as the otter-board and about 30cm in diameter (Illus 21).

Where there are no strong currents, in lakes and in areas such as the 'Baltic, modifications of the fyke net are used; the very large structures used in the Baltic are called 'pound nets'. These nets consist essentially of curtains of leader-net which obstruct the passage of the eels and guide them into the trap. One end of the curtain is attached at the shore or close to it. As in the case of the summer fyke, the length of the leader is critical. Sooner or later the eels swimming along it may decide to change their direction; even a slight deviation could easily take them past the trap. However, since the migrating eels are trying to move in one direction only at any particular point, the leaders can be very much longer than those used in the summer fykes where the eels are swimming at random. As the eels in a lake travel over a wide front, the pound nets must extend over a great distance. They are usually set in series with traps at intervals along the leader.

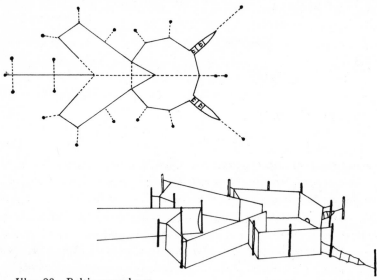

Illus 22   Baltic pound net

Since many eels migrate in mid-water, or at least some distance above the bottom, low leaders of the kind used in the summer fykes will do little to stop them. It may be said, though, that some silver eels are caught by fykes with such leaders and there are clandestine fisheries which use them with limited success. In general, a leader designed to guide silver eels must extend from the bed of the lake or sea to a little way *above* the surface. Determined migrating eels are well able to swim over a net which is level with the surface.

126

The design of pound nets can best be shown by diagrams as in Illus 22. The most striking point about the variations is the complexity of the arrangements. Clearly, it is not enough simply to obstruct the eels and lead them to a trap. The devices consisting of two or three traps or of blind pockets in the nets are apparently necessary to bewilder an astute eel which has reservations about taking the first route out of the maze which would lead it straight into the trap. In Chapter 4, page 73, the possibility that migrating eels try to keep some distance apart from each other was mentioned. If this is the case, it might go some way towards explaining why the silver-eel traps must be so very complex. If one or a few eels have entered the trap early in the course of the evening's run, their presence could well inhibit the free entry of more. These eels would then seek other exits from the parlour, and would only force their way in amongst those already in the trap when their search had failed.

The leaders and traps of the large nets are more or less permanent structures, supported on stakes, frequently with guy-lines attached to anchors to give added support. In the Baltic the nets may be as much as 6m deep and the leaders 600m or more in length.

Independently of the European developments of nets and grids, the Maoris of New Zealand had constructed elaborate eel-fishing equipment on much the same principles. In narrow rivers, up to about 12m wide, V-shaped guiding fences of wooden stakes were used. These led to conical nets which in turn led to *hinaki* or baskets with funnel-openings. In larger rivers, series of fences were built at an angle to the current, each fence leading to a funnel trap. The catch was emptied into a canoe. The eel or *tuna* was a very important food-fish for the Maoris and plays a major part in their mythology.

ELVERS

The principal elver fisheries of the world are on the Severn in England and the Loire in France. The methods used are extremely simple. Since the migrating elvers swim close to the bank, it is possible for the fishermen to scoop them out with a long-handled dip net. Wood is the traditional material for handle and frame, but redundant aluminium television aerials are becoming popular. Fishing takes place when the tide is rising after dark.

About ninety fishermen operate on the Severn and the annual catch may be as high as 50 tons. The best prices are offered by fishery authorities buying live elvers for stocking. When the demand for these is too low the elvers are sold for food. Elvers, fried with a little bacon, are extremely popular locally, and there is an export trade mainly to south-western Europe and Latin-American countries, particularly Mexico.

In Ireland all elvers caught are used for stocking upstream lakes although on the river Feale in Kerry fried elvers were once eaten. On the Feale the nets used to have short handles and the frames are about the same size as tennis rackets.

Dip-net fishing comes to an end in May when the elvers have lost their transparent appearance. Apparently they are much better able to avoid the nets at this stage. A new form of elver trap was devised in Germany by H. Koops and modified for use in conditions of low river-flows by Donal O'Leary in Ireland. This trap depends on the fact that elvers swim into a gentle flow of water in preference to trying to head into a strong current passing over rapids or waterfalls. The 'low head' trap is fully described by Donal O'Leary in an EIFAC paper.

It consists essentially of a nylon brush about 30cm wide by $1\frac{1}{2}$m in length. The brush forms the base of a wooden channel. The base-board of the brush is left free of bristles at its upper and lower ends. Water enters the channel through a slit at the upper end and flows over the bare board at considerable speed, too fast for the elvers to swim against. When the water meets the nylon tufts, the flow is broken and the elvers are able to swim or wriggle up the base-board through the brush. At the top of the brush, just above the tufts, a groove is cut in the base-board and this leads to a pipe at the side. When the elvers meet the full current of water they get diverted by it down the groove, into the pipe and so to a holding tank beside the trap. This trap can catch over 60kg of elvers in an hour when a good run is in progress. Eel of up to 40cm are also caught.

The brush system also works well simply as a pass to help elvers over a dam. Other materials including small stones, heather, twigs, or ropes twisted from hay, are all used to attract and either catch elvers or give them a safe passage over waterfalls.

The capture of elvers, or even the assistance given to their passage, leads away from the principle of hunting to that of artificial control of stocks. Sooner or later the hunter progresses towards the life of the farmer. Fishermen are the last of the great hunters, and even they are beginning to retire from their decidedly haphazard vocation. With the growing demand for high-quality animal protein, eel culture has begun to develop on a major scale and forms the subject of the next chapter.

6

FARMING EELS

The high price of eel flesh makes the idea of eel farming attractive. It has become a major industry in Japan since it began there in 1894 and is developing in other warm countries of the Far East. In Europe on the other hand, intensive eel farming exists only on a minute scale and will probably continue that way. The reason is the simple fact that the eel's optimum temperature is of the order of 24°C and, in Europe, few natural waters reach this or maintain it for long periods. At lower temperatures the time taken to reach marketable size is too long for an economic crop to be raised. It would probably take four or five years at least to grow market eels in the north-west of Europe. This might be tolerable if it entailed no more than caring for the eels during the month or two in which they grew actively, but intensively kept animals cannot be left to their own devices and a cool-climate eel farm would require maintenance over a long unproductive period every year.

The only serious possibility that exists is the establishment of an eel farm using the warm-water effluent of a power station. Here the fact that eels can survive periods of starvation would be an advantage. The stock would not be lost when the power station was out of service and no warm water available. Probably the greatest drawback would be the need for the fish farm to be large enough to pay the salaries of the highly qualified staff required to run it. It is possible for relatively unskilled people to herd cattle or sheep, since these animals live under fairly natural conditions; fish farms operate under artificial conditions and the risks of serious losses from disease or malnutrition are considerable. Food, water-quality and health of stock need ceaseless skilled attention.

The only viable eel farm I know of in western Europe is in the Mosel Valley in Germany and it operates in an extraordinary situation. The valley is one of the warmest in the country – the sun that warms the water also produces the most wonderful wine. The owner of the farm operates eel nets on the river a short distance from his farm and his nets catch, besides eels, a large quantity of other fish of little value. These fish can, however, be kept in cold store or be minced up and fed direct to the eels. Therefore the necessary high-protein feed is available as a by-product and the costs of transporting it are minimal.

Eel farming may possibly be developed in the south of France or in other Mediterranean countries where the temperature should be high enough. In recent years experiments have been made and abandoned, but suitable sites may yet be found. Much depends on the availability of food material. Practically no animal protein goes to waste nowadays. Mink farmers, fish farmers, fertiliser manufacturers and others, all compete for the raw material. Probably the greatest disadvantage the potential fish farmer is exposed to is that his establishment must have a large supply of suitable water. Other intensive farmers and factory owners are not so restricted, and can set themselves up close to the supply of raw materials.

Conditions are very different in the south of Japan at about 35° N latitude. The principal centre lies south-west of Tokyo and most of the farms are situated close to the sea. There the temperature in summer rises as high as 30°C and adequate water is available. Similar conditions can be found in Taiwan and Korea where eel farming is also developing. Japanese eel-farming methods have been lucidly described in a handbook by Atsushi Usui, a professional eel farmer. The book, in a translation by Ichiro Hayashi adapted by Gordon Williamson, was published in 1974 by Fishing News (Books) Ltd. With such a book in print there is no point in producing another instruction manual, and this chapter therefore is written simply as a description of the very interesting system used in Japan. Readers interested in practical details should refer to Usui.

The essential requirement of all fish-pond farming is an adequate supply of oxygen in the water. Water becomes saturated with oxygen at a concentration of the order of ten parts per million – the exact value depends on the temperature. That is to say, water cannot contain more than this very small quantity. Very active fish such as trout may die when the concentration falls to about half the saturation value. Eels can in fact survive much lower levels of oxygen, but they cannot feed actively under such circumstances.

Oxygen can be supplied to the water physically by diffusion at the surface. This takes place very slowly in still water but rapidly when the surface is broken – a mountain stream always has a high oxygen level. In fish ponds the oxygen uptake can be increased either by using a compressor to drive a stream of bubbles into the water or by some sort of splashing machine – either a pump or a rotating paddle to raise the water and let it splash back into the pond. In trout farming the usual technique is to supply the ponds with a large flow of fresh stream-water.

The other source of oxygen for water is biological, through the activity of green plants, mainly microscopic algae. These release oxygen in daylight as a by-product of photosynthesis. The activity of plants is not necessarily good for such fish as trout since the plants take up oxygen at night and may reduce the level dangerously. Trout may succumb to this, but eels are well able to rest during the danger period and revive when daylight brings the oxygen back. The oxygen in the water is used up not only by the respiration of the fish but also by the decay of their waste products, of the algal plants when they die, and of any uneaten food.

The typical trout farm uses a running-water system in which the pond water is changed several times a day thereby removing the waste products as well as supplying fresh oxygen. In Japan there is not enough running water available for all the eel farms and therefore a system of 'still-water' ponds is used. In these there is a slow supply of water which changes only about one-twentieth of the pond water each day. Running water tends to sweep away any algae which develop. In the still-water system the algal growth is encouraged and is the primary supplier of oxygen.

Water for the eel ponds in Japan usually comes from boreholes and has a steady temperature of 15° to 20°C. This is too cold for effective eel culture, but it warms up quickly in the ponds which are about 1m deep. In warm summer weather temperatures of 25° to 30°C are maintained. Shallow water and bright weather allow the production of dense blooms of phytoplankton. The quantity of plankton is not constant but follows a regular cycle, reaching a peak about every forty days. At that stage the water looks like pea soup. After the peak the plants die and it may be necessary to flush out the ponds to prevent the accumulation of decaying material.

From time to time planktonic animals invade the ponds. They feed on the plants, thereby reducing the oxygen production, and they themselves consume some of the oxygen both while alive and in decaying after they die. Some forms, such as the water fleas, can be killed by chemical methods. Others, like the rotifers, have to be washed out by a complete change of the pond water.

In many farms each pond is provided with a 'resting corner'. This is a walled-off portion of the pond which the eels can enter through a narrow slit. The water is either circulated rapidly or aerated mechanically, and the eels are able to swim in for relief if the oxygen level in the main pond falls uncomfortably low.

A complete eel farm has four sizes of ponds : small and large elver tanks and two types of pond for bigger eels. The elver tanks are usually built in glasshouses and the water may also be heated artificially. This part of the rearing takes place in winter and spring. Natural water is warm enough for wild elvers to thrive in, but their growth at winter temperatures is too slow for the fish-farmer's demands.

The elvers' first home is a circular concrete tank of 5m

diameter with water up to 60cm deep. It is aerated by water which is sprayed on the surface by a series of jets. The jets are directed so that a circular current is maintained and the water drains through a pipe in the centre. At this stage the elvers want to swim against a current and presumably the circular motion satisfies them. The elvers introduced to these ponds are about 6cm long and weigh on average 0.16g. The stocking rate in the tank is about 400g per square metre – 50,000 elvers to each.

As many as half the elvers may die in the first month, a high figure but probably very much lower than natural mortality in rivers where birds and fish take an enormous toll. At the end of the month the elvers are caught, sorted out into two sizes, and transferred to the second elver tanks. Keeping the fast and slow growers separate helps the slow ones on. In fish, to say nothing of human communities, the most vigorous individuals take the best food and the less aggressive ones tend to starve. Removal of the top class in this way creates a new hierarchy amongst the weaker fraction, and they can recover some of their lost ground.

In the second pond the stocking density is much lower, about 100g per square metre. The elvers stay there for a month. By this time they have reached a length of 12cm and are ready for regrading and transfer to the first of the outdoor ponds. These, the 'fingerling ponds', are rectangular, excavated in the earth with mud bottoms and concrete sides. They have an area of up to 300sq m and depth of 1m. The pond edge has to have an overhanging lip to prevent the elvers from wriggling out and straying in wet weather.

By June or July the fingerling are moved to the adult ponds. These are also rectangular, but may have a surface area of as much as 20,000sq m. Smaller ponds, down to 500sq m, are coming into use and even smaller and more intensive ones may develop. The smaller the pond, the more difficult and sophisticated the husbandry, but high production in a small area is possible.

The adult ponds have mud bottoms and the depth varies from

80cm at the inlet end to 120cm at the outlet, the sloping bed allowing complete drainage of the empty pond. The edges of the ponds are faced with concrete slats or stones. The outlet has a sluice arrangement which can be adjusted to allow drainage of either the bottom or the surface water of the pond. Usually the eel farm is surrounded by a canal at a lower level than the bottoms of the ponds into which all the drainage water flows.

By September the eels measure 20–30cm and are caught and graded for the last time. In their first summer they have increased from an average weight of 0.16g to as much as 60g, a fantastic rate compared with the development of a wild northern European eel which might weigh $\frac{1}{2}$g at the end of the same period.

The second season of the farm-eels' life begins in April when a temperature of 12°C brings them out of hibernation. They are fed once a day and are expected to reach market size of 150–200g in the autumn. They are sold during the winter months. Production of market fish for a year in 1,000sq m of pond is of the order of 4 tons. This requires stocking of 10kg of elvers, perhaps 60,000 individuals.

At the end of 1973, Professor Yamamoto and Dr K. Yamamuchi in Hokkaido University took the great step of artificially fertilising and hatching the eggs of *Anguilla japonica.* This was the first time that freshwater eels had been successfully spawned and also the first time that undoubted eel eggs had been hatched. However, this attainment is a long way from being the beginning of the production of elvers for stocking. Between hatching and reaching the elver stage the larvae have to make their ocean migration, and it seems likely that simulating this under farm conditions will be difficult.

The natural run of elvers therefore remains the sole source of supply of elvers for the farms. In Japan the annual demand is for about 100 tons of elvers and this quantity can rarely if ever be supplied locally. According to Usui in 1972 only 10 tons were obtained from Japan. European elvers were imported in quantity, no less than 64 tons from France and 8 tons from England. French elvers come mainly from the Loire and English from the Severn, both being rivers where there are no important fisheries for grown eels and where the majority of elvers which escape the nets are liable to die before reaching maturity.

Although the elvers are small and delicate they can survive for some time out of water. For transport overland they are placed on perforated wooden trays in boxes. The trays are stacked and the top one may be filled with ice which melts and allows a steady trickle of cool water to pass over the captives. Elvers for Japan are dispatched by air-freight and packed in polystyrene boxes.

The elvers take about four days to settle down after being moved to the tanks. In daytime they hide under stones, emerging only at night and they take no interest in food. Feeding can begin over the next week, and mashed-up earthworms are recommended as a starting diet. The elvers take little notice of this material unless they actually bump into it. Even then they don't snap it up but seem to try biting everything around them. Eventually, by a process of trial and error, they find and swallow the food.

In the course of a week they become more highly skilled in finding the food and are ready to be trained to come to a particular feeding place. The food for the first fortnight is a paste of minced earthworm or bivalve flesh, later *Tubifex* worms may be added, and afterwards minced fish-flesh or artificial feed is offered. This is placed on a gauze tray and held just below the surface of the water. As soon as the elvers have had enough the tray is removed, so that no waste feed can foul the tank. In the course of each day when the water is warm they consume 25 per cent of their body weight in food.

The larger eels are fed only once a day, usually in the morning. The technique is quite different from that used in trout farms where the food is scattered in the water. The eel food is offered at the same time in the same place and, as with the elvers, removed from the pond as soon as the eels have eaten enough. Their habit of assembling at the feeding point is used subsequently when they have to be caught : the whole population of a pond can easily be surrounded by a net. In warm weather they eat about 10 per cent of their body weight daily.

Farm eels are fed either on fresh fish or on artificial feed. The feed is sold in powder form and consists largely of fish meal with added carbohydrate. The protein content is about 52 per cent. The powder is mixed with water and up to 10 per cent of vitamin oil, to form a paste which is placed on a mesh tray in the pond. The fishes used are species such as mackerel, *Scomber*, sand eel, *Ammodytes* and sardine, *Sardinops*, species with a high fat content in the flesh. The fresh fishes are threaded on a wire through the eyes and dipped in boiling water which softens the skin. They are then lowered into the pond and the eels eat off the flesh in about five minutes. When the meal is over, the heads and bones of the fodder fish are removed. Apparently the eels are quick to learn to recognise the smell of the cooked food, quite an achievement for a species which normally insists on living on very freshly killed prey. In the eel farm in the Mosel the eels were ready to eat freshly caught fish, but frozen food had to be flavoured with fresh blood to attract them.

The conversion rate of fresh fish as eel food is 7 : 1 and of the artificial feed 1.4 : 1. That means it takes 7kg of fish or 1.4kg of artificial fodder to produce 1kg of eels. There is not, in fact, much discrepancy between the figures, since fish has a moisture content of the order of 70 per cent by weight while meal contains only about 10 per cent water. From a storage point of view the dry meal is much more satisfactory and also easier to feed but, in eel farms situated close to a fishing-port, fresh fish may be much cheaper. However, eels are creatures of habit and do not take kindly to having their diet changed abruptly.

Even in southern Japan winters are cool, and the pond-water temperature from December to February is less than 9°C. No food at all is given in this season. Feeding at a very low rate begins in March when the temperature rises to 11 °C. The peak months are August and September when temperatures are over 23°, and more than half the entire food supply is provided in this short period. The high rate of feeding is required partly because in the warm water the eels are digesting their food much more rapidly, but also because they have grown bigger and the total weight of eels in the farm is approaching its yearly maximum. In October the temperature has fallen below the critical level of 23° and, in spite of the large quantity of eels, the food requirements have fallen to little more than half the September figure.

The fully grown eels are caught for market either by using a scoop net at their feeding place, by drawing a seine net through the pond or by collecting them at the outlet pipe by tying a net bag about 3m long over it. They must be starved before transport so that the guts are completely emptied. This process takes up to three days. One method is to put the eels in perforated plastic tubs through which water is allowed to trickle. Another is to place them in plastic baskets which are suspended in the ponds above the bottom, or placed in concrete raceways in a stream of water. If the eels are not starved they foul the boxes or tanks in which they are being carried, and many may die on the journey. Well packed eels can survive for at least one or two days.

Such is the work of a complete eel-rearing unit. Many farms however undertake only a part of the process. Some specialise in elver rearing and sell their stock as fingerling. This phase of the development can be completed in a relatively small space, but calls for much more intensive work than the later growing. Other farms specialise in buying the fingerling and rearing them to market size.

Intensive eel culture seems likely to develop in the near future in east Africa and Australia. In Europe and North America, however, the low temperatures of natural waters allow little hope for progress. That is not to say that artificial production of eels is not a very interesting and important undertaking. The prin-

ciple is to assist elvers or young eels in moving them into productive waters, to allow them to develop at their normal rate,
eating natural food, and then to control the capture of the stock.

The greatest drawback to eel stocking in northern countries
is the very long time which must elapse before results can be
seen. This makes experimental work extremely difficult, and
recommendations for rates of stocking depend largely, if not
entirely, on informed guesswork. A rate of 400 elvers per ha is
one recommendation. In Lough Neagh elvers have been caught
at the mouth of the river Bann and moved overland for many
years. An average of 26 million are taken up to Lough Neagh
every year and the output of the lake is of the order of 700
tons, perhaps 2 million eels. The area of Lough Neagh is nearly
40,000ha which gives a stocking rate of 750 elvers per ha, and
an annual production of about 50 eels per ha. What is not
known is whether this rate is high, low or optimal.

The biggest and probably the oldest eel-culture establishment
in Europe is at the lagoon of Comacchio on the Adriatic, not
far from Venice. The area of water there is of the order of
80,000ha. This is divided into about fifteen inter-connected
lakes in which the levels of the water can be regulated by sluices.
The depth is about 1m and there is high productivity of
invertebrates and small fish which the eels feed on.

In winter the sluices are kept shut as far as possible so that
the water level rises and the salinity drops. In spring, at the
time of the elver run, the sluices are opened so that the fresh
water runs out to the sea and attracts elvers and other species of
fish. The sluices are closed again until autumn and, when they
are next opened, the silver eels try to escape. However, they are
led by a series of fences into a small pond from which they may
be taken by dip-nets. The production in a year can be as high as
1,000 tons.

Conditions for such controlled eel fishing are not so very
widely available. European eel culture therefore is largely a
matter of capturing elvers or small eels, transporting them overland to lakes or rivers to grow under natural conditions and

harvesting them by normal eel-fishing methods. This approach has long been followed in Germany where the rivers are too long to allow many eels to reach their upper waters. Even in Ireland where the longest river, the Shannon, is only 250km, the stocks of eels in upstream lakes are very small. In Ireland the limiting factor is not so much the length of the rivers but the fact that lakes are situated close to the river mouths. Ascending elvers find plenty of space in the downstream lakes and apparently settle there for long periods without making an effort to hurry on upstream.

On rivers like the Weser in Germany, the Feale and Maigue in Ireland, the Severn and the Loire, elvers are caught and stored in tanks, until sufficient have been collected to make up a load on a road tanker. About 17 tons of water on a lorry can hold 1 ton of elvers – 6 million little eels to a load. The storage tanks may be made of concrete, up to 2m deep and containing water to 1m. Elvers can climb up damp concrete walls to a height of about 50cm but fall off anything higher. Fibre-glass tanks are also used. The water is aerated by spraying with fine jets of water from a perforated pipe. In Ireland elvers for the river Shannon are stored in spare salmon-rearing tanks which have a large supply of fresh water flowing in through a 25mm pipe. These tanks are made of hard plastic material which the elvers are unable to climb. The water is about 10cm deep and the walls of the tanks 40cm high.

The elvers are released in the upstream lakes and left to their own devices. There must be some losses due to predation but in White Russia, according to V. Kokhnenko, examination of the stomachs of 2,000 large eels in a lake which had been stocked with elvers gave no evidence of cannibalism. Since the elvers are nocturnal and most other lake-dwelling fish hunt by day, the chances of survival of the young eels are good. Cormorants and herons and other birds certainly take a toll of small eels but there may well be a tendency for these birds to select eels which have been forced by overcrowding to hunt in daylight. At the time the elvers are planted in lakes the temperature is usually too low for larger eels to be active. This gives the elvers some time in which to move around and spread out from the dense concentration which would leave them vulnerable to heavy predation by their own species. It is possible also that they seek different feeding grounds from the larger eels and so avoid them.

In the river Shannon in 1960 a programme for stocking the lakes with elvers and small eels was begun. When the first survey of the yellow eels was made in a lake on the system in 1969 it was possible to make an assessment of the stock before the effect of planting was apparent, since hardly any eels of less than 10 years old were caught in the nets. When the same portion of the lake was next sampled, five years later, the effects of the elver transport could be seen very clearly : there were about three times as many eels in the shallows. What was more, many eels were found in deeper water where hardly any had been caught before. Even fifteen years after the first stocking it was too early to assess the final results, since all the eels in the commercial catches are silvers and few reach the silver stage in less than fifteen years in the river system. In such situations there is no serious possibility of making controlled experiments – the chances are that any manager or research scientist will be dead or moved to another job long ,before a proper assessment can be made. Scrupulous keeping of records combined with regular monitoring, however, will give some indications of the effectiveness of the undertaking. For example in Hungary, where there are no native eels, it was found that eels grew to maturity in as little as six years.

Ideally, as well as monitoring the numbers and sizes of eels in an experimentally stocked lake, studies of the abundance of the food organisms should be made. Taken over the years this would indicate whether the eel population was being increased to too high a level. Where this cannot be done, valuable information can be collected by analysing the stomach contents of samples of eels. The depletion of any favoured food organisms would soon become apparent.

In spite of the difficulties of assessing the results, it is obvious that the production rates of wild eels can be greatly increased by stocking programmes. In this early stage of the proceedings the difficulties are more serious in the eyes of the fishery biologists than in the view of the fishery manager. In time, demands for elvers of the order of those made by the Japanese eel farmers will make their cost a matter for serious consideration. When that happens something better than a guess will be needed to determine the numbers of elvers to be planted in each lake.

7

EELS FOR EATING

Bringing eels to the consumer is a specialised undertaking. With very few exceptions the quality of fishes as food deteriorates as soon as they die. Salmon and trout have a relatively long 'shelf life', taste good one or two days after capture and may still be eatable for a further day or so. Other freshwater fishes are best eaten within hours of death and this is true of the eel.

However, eels which are kept cool and moist can be kept alive for days out of water and the traditional procedure for fishermen has been to keep and sell their catches alive. Eels which die shortly after capture are usually dumped by the small-scale fisherman – a habit which does not exactly endear them to sport fishermen in the same regions. The sight of a few dozen eel corpses in the sparkling clear water of a lake is none too encouraging at the start of a day's angling.

KEEP-NETS AND BOXES

The usual practice in Ireland and many other countries is for the fisherman to keep his catch alive for up to a week. He then either packs and ships them himself, or else sells to a travelling merchant who makes a regular round of the fishermen.

For short periods, up to twenty-four hours, eels can be kept alive in a netting container, such as the cod-end of a fyke net, suspended in the water or resting on the bottom of an unpolluted river or lake. The smaller eels, however, will make considerable efforts to escape by forcing their tails through the mesh. Sometimes they succeed in enlarging an opening sufficiently and then

Illus 23 At fishing and marketing stations, eels are kept in large floating boxes until needed for consumption. Here is seen the handling and storage of eels at Lough Neagh in Ireland.

bigger individuals can get to work, leaving a broken and empty net. Even if the mesh holds, the eels will damage their tails in the process. This allows a fungus infection to develop which may be fatal.

Another risk in leaving such a bag of eels on the bottom is that local pockets of water with a dangerously low oxygen content may exist. This can occur in a bay or an estuary in which eels thrive and can be caught. The wild eels can avoid the dangerous areas but the caged ones have no escape. This has happened only once in my experience. A fisherman who was trying a new area and had done very well lost his entire catch overnight close to where he had caught them.

The most widely used method of storing live eels is to keep them in floating wooden boxes. The size of the box is of no great importance provided the eels are not overcrowded. It is the floor space rather than the depth of the box that matters. The eels will spend most of their time resting on the floor and should be given plenty of room. Several layers of captive eel on the bottom of the box will not be very comfortable.

The boxes must be very strongly made. Eels will force their tails into any slits between the boards, and try to enlarge the opening. If the construction is not very secure an eel can force the boards apart. The corners of the boxes can be strengthened with metal and the whole box surrounded with metal strips. The lid of the eel box is an opening in the top, big enough to allow the catch to be poured in quickly so that none escape over the edges. Large boxes are emptied by a hand net and the openings must allow plenty of room for this operation (Illus 23).

While there must be no slits or holes which the eels can enter to damage the box or themselves, there must be plenty of openings to allow the water to circulate freely. A collection of eels in stagnant water in warm weather quickly reduces the oxygen content to a dangerous level and novice fishermen quite often lose their catches. The wood may be perforated with holes of 1cm diameter or less, or windows of expanded metal may be made in the sides. These have to be surrounded by firmly fixed strips of wood so that the eels don't damage their tails on the cut edges of the grille.

These boxes are left floating near the shore on lakes or large rivers, in sheltered bays where they are not disturbed by wave action. Where there are silver-eel fisheries on large river systems and catches of the order of several tons may be made in a night, more substantial containers are used. On the river Corrib in Galway, large wooden cages supported by steel girders are fixed to the river bed, sheltered from the main rush of water by the pillars of a bridge (Illus 19). The cages have metal-mesh windows in the sides. At Killaloe on the river Shannon, the fishery office building is supported on stilts over the river. Water flows through

Illus 24 Eel transporter, with tanks and apparatus for circulating water. Some merchants prefer to blow compressed air into the tanks through diffusers

the lower storeys and the eels are kept in open-topped cages suspended at the surface.

TRANSPORT AND STORAGE

For transport on a grand scale, juggernaut road tankers are used for eels. These have been developed in Holland and elsewhere and may carry as much as 15 tons of eel in 15 tons of water. The lorry is a flat truck with a number of separate rectangular tanks (Illus 24). These are filled through a top opening and fitted with a door at the bottom for emptying. A compressor on the lorry bubbles air through the water, and this is enough to keep the eels alive and well for at least four days. On very long journeys the water is changed at 4-day intervals. Eels in these lorries can be transported by sea in drive-on ferries as easily as they can be taken by road. American eels are brought alive to Europe in this way.

This scale of operation is all very well for fisheries the size of Lough Neagh, the IJsselmeer or those in the south of France or Italy. But a large proportion of the eel catch comes from much smaller sources. In these cases a traditional container is a wooden box holding five shallow trays. The floors of the trays are made of thin wood, perforated with holes about ½cm in diameter. The four lower trays are filled with eels but the top one contains ice. This melts slowly and the cool water drips continually over the eels, keeping them moist. Provided its skin is damp an eel can respire out of the water. One such box contains 128lb (57.6kg) of eels. Eels in these boxes are regularly sent from the remotest parts of the west of Ireland by rail and road to Billingsgate market where they arrive in good condition one or two days later.

An alternative method of transporting small quantities of eels is widely used in Japan. The eels are placed with some ice in a polythene bag which is then inflated with oxygen and tied. Each bag holds 10kg of eels and is packed for greater security first inside a second bag and then in a cardboard container. This system keeps the eels for thirty hours or more and has the advantage of being suitable for air freight. Wooden boxes are too heavy and too liable to leak for air transport.

Since the silver eels can readily adapt to salt water, another method of sea transport is in 'well boats'. The eels are kept in the holds in salt-water tanks which can easily be pumped out and replaced with fresh sea water. At Maldon in Essex, England, a special barge has been developed which combines transport and storage. It has perforated sides and bottom to allow water circulation and can store 60 tons of eels. Every two weeks the barge is towed downstream into the sea and the eels are given a salt-water bath for two hours. This treatment prevents some diseases. *Saprolegnia*, the fungus which attacks injured skin in all kinds of fish, can be killed or at least inhibited by sea water. Several other fungus diseases also respond to this treatment.

Large-scale storage of eels is very often based on a large number of relatively small boxes rather than a small number of large tanks. Provided space is not expensive, the smaller units are much more satisfactory since an outbreak of disease can be easily controlled without damaging the entire stock. Eels in the wild may be healthy, but the stress of being confined to a small space and perhaps frequently handled lessens their resistance to infection.

Eel merchants try to avoid keeping yellow eels for long periods. They do not have such great fat reserves as the silvers and lose weight and condition much more quickly. Also the fact that they are normally caught and handled in warm weather means that they are very active in captivity and use up their reserves. Silver eels on the other hand are caught and kept at lower temperatures and are, in any case, adapted to withstand a long period of starvation. They can therefore be kept for several months in good condition.

Silver-eel fishermen who had good storage facilities used to make a point of holding onto their catches until January or later, marketing them when the supply had fallen and prices risen. The problem was to decide just when the loss of weight or wastage by death led to a diminishing return. Since cold storage has become more easily available this practice is no longer so popular.

Dead eels may be shipped for short distances simply chilled with ice. For longer storage, eels are best allowed to die in pans in a cold room. This is probably the most humane way of dispatching them, the gradual lowering of the temperature simply reduces their activity until they pass to a torpid state. When immobilised or dead, but still soft, the eels can either be treated individually or packed in boxes which contain about 40kg. They are quick-frozen to minus $20\,^{\circ}$C and dipped in cold water. The latter process, called 'glazing', gives the eels a protective coating of ice which reduces the rate of spoiling by oxidation. The glazed blocks can be wrapped in polythene and stored in cardboard containers. Storage for as much as six months is satisfactory after this treatment.

EEL COOKERY

The freshwater eel is regarded by those prepared to try it as one of the most delectable of fish. The relationship of human to eel is polarised : many people express revulsion and refuse to touch it; those who have once taken the plunge become addicted.

On fieldwork in summer I bring a deep-frying pan, some vegetable oil and a supply of flour. Specimens, preferably between 50 and 60cm long, which have been duly weighed, measured and recorded, are each evening gutted, skinned and chopped in steaks between 1 and 2cm thick. The steaks are shaken up in some flour and fried in the oil for between five and ten minutes, until golden brown. Crispy and succulent they are the great reward for a day's fishing.

This is the simplest way I know of preparing eels and one of the best. It is very popular in Holland and elsewhere in northern Europe, indeed I learnt it from a Dutch fisherman. Unfortunately there is a little more to it than the last paragraph suggests. A problem which all eel fishermen meet is the need to dispatch the victim. Decapitation certainly kills an eel but it does not immobilise it : the body continues to wriggle with all the vigour of life and also produces slime. Skinning and gutting such a beast is almost impossible. Killing eels by chilling has been mentioned – in a polythene bag in a refrigerator is a good way – but this is not always practicable.

The most widely used method of killing eels is to put them in a deep bucket or bin and cover them with salt. They react to the salt by releasing large quantities of slime and the loss of slime prevents their breathing. All are dead and relaxed in one or two hours. The slime can be scraped off, an essential part of the procedure if the eels are to be smoked, since eels for smoking are not skinned.

When gutting eels it is important to remember that the kidney and gonads extend back for some distance behind the vent. The body cavity is therefore opened by stabbing with a pointed knife about 2cm behind the vent and cutting forward as far as the

149

head. The viscera can then be removed by scraping with the knife.

Eels can be skinned quickly and easily after a great deal of practice. It is hard work for a part-timer. I have tried various methods and seen others demonstrated and find the following the most satisfactory. The knife should be sharp and pointed, with a blade of about 15cm. The only other requirement is a supply of clean sawdust or newspaper, used to grip eel or skin. Make a small transverse cut through the skin on the back, just behind the head. The knife is inserted through this and used to separate skin from muscle on one side of the eel, the important point being to leave the skin attached to the head. Having removed the skin down about 2cm of the body, it is possible to turn the knife and cut through the muscle and backbone down as far as the skin on the opposite side, again being careful not to cut through the skin.

The body is now attached to the head by skin only and you have a flap of muscle on one side from which the skin has been removed. Grip the muscle in one hand, using sawdust or paper if necessary. Take the head in the other hand and pull in opposite directions. If all is well the skin will peel off like a recalcitrant glove. Sometimes the skin breaks in the process, an especially dangerous point is near the vent. When this happens the knife must be used to separate enough skin to grip and pull again. Once the skin is removed the eel makes an attractive piece of meat, clean, grey and free from slime.

Probably more eels are eaten smoked than any other way. They are killed either by salting or freezing. After thawing the slime must be removed, and can quite easily be scraped off with a blunt knife. The eels are gutted but not skinned or beheaded since they are suspended in the smoking kiln by a skewer thrust through the head. Commercial smoking will be described later, but home or even field smoking is simple and satisfactory. Since I bought the portable smoking oven made by the Swedish firm of Abu, I have enjoyed smoked eel as a change from deep-fried on my fishing trips.

The Abu oven is a metal box 30 x 15cm by 8cm deep. It has a loose sliding lid which allows the air to escape as it heats, but which prevents the free circulation of air which would make the sawdust used burn rather than char. The heat is provided by a methylated spirit (wood alcohol) burner.

The floor of the box is sprinkled with sawdust. Oak or beech are preferred but most hardwoods will be satisfactory. Softwoods in general have too much resin and this imparts a very strong flavour to the fish. Fishing-tackle dealers sell packets of suitable sawdust and this is often the most convenient way of getting it. Once I collected a supply of coarser chips made when a chainsaw had been used to fell a beech tree. The chips were fresh and damp but worked perfectly well. The idea of using eel from the lake and wood from the forest beside it was particularly satisfying.

The eels, cut in lengths to fit in the box, are soaked in brine for ten minutes or rubbed with a little salt. They are then placed on a grille in the box, which keeps them out of contact with the sawdust. The whole cooking process is complete in about ten minutes and the eels are good hot or may be left to cool. Wrapped in polythene they keep well in a deep-freeze.

Although it is very convenient for preparing a single meal, the Abu kiln is not suitable for handling quantities of eels. I therefore developed a larger machine, capable of taking about ten eels at a time. It was a metal drum measuring 40cm high by 30cm diameter, open at the top. A bigger one would probably be better. Sawdust was sprinkled on the bottom, to a depth of a few millimetres. The eels were too long for the drum and had to be cut in two; they were then skewered through the head or through the trunk. The oven was covered with aluminium foil and set on top of a gas cooker, burning at a low flame.

The first experiment was not entirely successful. Half an hour's smoking resulted in a delicious smell and a tasty firm-fleshed product. But it left an unpleasantly strong aftertaste which indicated a need for longer cooking. At the end of another half-hour a sound of frying issued from the apparatus. All the eels except one had fallen off their skewers and were roasting in the sawdust. The remaining one was perfect, and the bits of the fallen specimens which could be cleared of charred wood were also good. Next time I consulted the instruction book, prepared by the British Torry Research Station in Aberdeen, home of the finest smoked herring.

Among other recommendations which I had not known about was the advice to smoke for one hour at 35°C, half an hour at 50° and one hour at 73°. This allows for a gradual and even drying of the eels before the cooking sets in. Unfortunately I found myself at home with kiln, eels and no thermometer. So I judged the temperature by hand : for the first hour the sides of the oven were kept warm, for the next half-hour about as hot as could be comfortably held, and for the final hour too hot to touch in comfort. Apart from the loss of one or two eels off the skewers the results were very satisfactory. I had used kebab skewers of about 2mm diameter which must have been able to cut through the softened flesh. The books recommend a much heavier rod, wooden or metal, diameter about 5mm.

This process was developed for commercial work using the 'Torry' kiln in which temperature and other conditions can be very accurately controlled. The principle, however, is that the entire drying and cooking procedures take place in the smoke. A different system was developed in the Dutch Fishery Research Institute in IJmuiden and has been used successfully in Ireland. The kiln is fired by gas jets and has a steam generator attached. It is heated to 110°C before the eels are inserted. The temperature drops as soon as they are put in and is brought back to over 90°, after which some steam is introduced. About 3 minutes of steam treatment makes the bellies of the eels gape wide apart. They are then cooked at between 90° and 115° for between 10 and 30 minutes – cool and short cooking for small eels, long and hot for big. Wood chips in a wire basket are then set on fire and damped down with peat dust or with more sawdust, and the smouldering basket is placed in the kiln.

The smoke production must be watched to make sure that the chips do not blaze up, flames being damped with more sawdust. The main heat supply is still the gas jets and the smoking process lasts for anything between 15 and 40 minutes, again depending on the size of the eels.

Detailed information on smoking can usually be had from national fishery institutes. It is quite obvious from the difference between the two methods outlined here that there is no single perfect method and, in fact, techniques vary from country to country, even from region to region. There is room for endless experiment. Perhaps the most important point is to record the sequence used so that the most suitable way can be repeated after its discovery.

In some countries large eels are preferred for smoking, in others small ones are considered suitable. Silver eels of any size will smoke well but small yellows, less than 45cm or so, are useless. Their fat content is low and smoking dries out the meat to too great a degree. Gutting and smoking together reduce the weight of an eel by about 40 per cent.

Smoked eels are usually eaten without any further treatment. The skin peels off easily, and they can be served either whole or filleted. For variety, smoked-eel paté is an excellent dish. Add the juice of a lemon to 1lb (0.5kg) of fillets of smoked eel and leave them to soak overnight. Mince the eel and stir it with salt, pepper, paprika and $\frac{1}{2}$lb (0.2kg) of softened butter to make a smooth and delicious paste.

Besides the methods of frying and smoking eel described above, boiling and baking are possible and strongly recommended. The cooking period is of the order of twenty minutes. Eel on its own has a good flavour but it also takes kindly to preparation with herbs or sauces. Many appetising recipes are given by Jane Grigson in *Fish Cookery* and most general cookery books provide a few ideas. Conger, although caught and marketed in large quantities, has a much less pleasant taste than freshwater eel, but it does have good firm flesh. The conger pikes on the other hand are considered very good and are caught in great quantities.

Pickled or marinated eel is excellent and very easy to prepare. The eel, skinned and cut in lengths of about 5cm is fried or grilled until golden brown. The marinade is basically vinegar to which treacle, sultanas, onion and various herbs are added. This is boiled for two minutes after which the eel is put in and the pickle brought back to the boil. That is all, it is ready to eat when cool and keeps well. For a 1lb (0.5kg) eel I used $\frac{1}{2}$ pint (0.25l) of red wine vinegar, a teaspoonful of treacle, about a dozen sultanas, half an onion sliced, a sprinkling of sage and a pinch of garlic salt. One could ring endless changes in the details.

Elvers may be eaten fried or in elver pies, but this destruction of undersized animals goes against all my principles.

Finally, there are a few highly specialised national approaches to eel cookery. The Maoris remove the backbone and dry the eels in the sun, keeping them for food in the winter. The traditional Japanese eel dish is called *kabayaki*. The eel is split in two, guts and backbone removed, and cut into pieces about 12cm long. Several skewers are inserted in each piece to prevent it from curling up. The pieces are cooked lightly over steam and then alternatively dipped in sauce and grilled about three times. The sauce, invariably with secret ingredients, is basically a mixture of soy sauce and sweet *sake* (rice beer) with a little sugar. It sounds very good.

Jellied eel may be bought on the roadside in London and the east of England. As with *kabayaki* the details are secret and vary from cook to cook. The eels are cleaned, gutted and chopped in pieces about 5cm long but not skinned – some of the jelly actually comes from the skin. The eels are boiled for ten minutes or more and cold water is added. This brings the oil to the surface from which it can be skimmed off. There may be enough jelly in the eels to make the whole preparation set when it cools, otherwise a solution of gelatine must be added. Herbs, spices and vinegar may all be brought in to taste. Clearly the jellying of eels is a matter which depends on experience and artistic skill.

In spite of their excellence as food, eels are still a relatively under-exploited fish. The production of east African fisheries is still remarkably low and there must surely be room for great developments in fishing for eels in many of the Indo-Pacific islands.

Fishing is usually developed by fishermen with or without government encouragement. Biologists come on the scene later and have a vital part to play in maintaining fisheries which are otherwise liable to damage by over-enthusiastic harvesting. The next chapter is a short practical one for the benefit of fishery scientists who may be told, as I was once, 'You do eels'.

8

INVESTIGATING EELS

The approach to most aspects of eel biology is the same as for other fishes. Conclusions are based on the study of relatively large samples by statistical treatment of measurements of length, weight and age, and analysis of the contents of the stomachs. However, in some respects eels need special treatment owing to difficulties in catching them and handling the specimens after capture. This chapter is not an attempt at a treatise on methods in fish biology, but an outline practical guide on manipulating eels.

The best principle for sampling fish is to use the methods favoured by professional fishermen. These have already been described in Chapter 5. My own study material has nearly all come from summer fyke nets. These nets work well in lakes from the shallows down to the 30m or so which is the greatest depth found in Ireland. There is no reason to believe that they would not be effective in deeper water. These nets also work well in rivers. In the interests of comfort, nets set in deep water should be attached to a relatively heavy rope, since a light rope cuts into the hands of the person hauling in the net. My standard unit of effort has been a train of eight nets, since this number can be packed into a large polythene bag and even when wet can be carried easily.

The nets are set to fish overnight. The time of day when they are set or collected seems to make little difference provided setting takes place at least an hour before sunset. Usually it is more convenient to empty the nets on board the boat. Plastic dustbins make ideal containers, but in a small boat space may require that buckets be used. Buckets should be as large as possible to prevent big eels from leaping out. I usually put about 1l of anaesthetic in each bucket. This reduces the eels' efforts to escape and leaves them ready for examination as soon as the catch is brought ashore. A cloth or any other cover for the bucket also helps to keep the eels quiet.

The anaesthetic is used in the interests both of humane treatment and of convenience. The most effective chemical in my experience is chlorbutol (1,1,1-trichloro-2-methylpropan-2-ol). It is supplied in crystalline form. About 5g or a lump the size of a plum stone can be dissolved in 1l of water to make a saturated solution. Other anaesthetics, such as MS 222, keep eels quiet enough to allow for weighing and measuring but apparently do not prevent them from reacting violently to being tagged or dissected. Often, individual eels will not react to the first exposure to a chlorbutol solution. They should be placed in a fresh mixture of it. It seems possible that the anaesthetic is neutralised by the slime of the eels.

Anaesthetised eels can be measured on a flat board with a ruler placed flush with the surface. A more convenient measuring board has a V-shaped groove about 10cm deep, with the ruler lying in the bottom of the V. Experience in Irish fisheries showed that measurements of a sample of about 100 eels caught in fyke nets gave a satisfactory picture of the population.

For studying the food, the best system is to cut out the stomach and squeeze its contents into a phial of 70 per cent alcohol. Formaline is a less expensive preservative but it hardens the food organisms, making them more difficult to examine. Whole stomachs can be placed in the alcohol, but it is easier to empty the stomach when fresh than after it has been preserved for a while. I found that a sample of 50 stomachs would give a good representation of the food of an eel population. Since about one-third of the stomachs will be empty this entails collecting 70 to 80 eels.

Finally there is the all-important matter of age determination. An international workshop of eel specialists was held in

Montpellier in France in 1975, and friendly but definite differences of opinion on the value of various methods was registered. The same body is continuing to study the subject in the hopes of adding greater precision to age readings. The only method which appears to be really reliable entails one or two days' work on each eel and therefore cannot be considered as practical.

The principle of age determination in fish is based on the fact that growth rings, resulting from the alternating periods of fast and slow growth in the life of temperate fish, are found in many parts of the skeleton. The problem is to find a structure which can be examined conveniently. Ehrenbaum and Marukawa (see page 47) established the use of the otolith in eel age-determination. For practical purposes the otoliths may be found by dividing the skull in two by a median cut, removing the brain, and searching with a forceps in a pair of cavities which lie off the floor of the skull to either side near the hind end. The otoliths are cleaned by rubbing between finger and thumb and stored as dry specimens.

The skulls of small eels can be divided into two with a strong dissecting scissors. Large specimens are less tractable because the bone is very hard. I use a surgeon's rib-cutting forceps to make the first cut, a little way behind the eyes and across the head (Illus 25). The next (median) cuts, one through the roof of the skull and one through the base and one or two of the vertebrae, can then be made with a scissors. After this the skull falls apart in two halves. For the biggest eels the rib-forceps is used for the median cuts as well.

While the growth rings in small otoliths can easily be seen when the specimen is immersed in creosotum, large otoliths are best treated by burning. The otolith is held in a bunsen flame on a scalpel blade for half a minute or slightly more. One or two cracks across the short axes can then be seen and, with a little gentle pressure with a needle, the otolith divides in two and the rings can be seen on the broken faces. The burned otoliths are very delicate but can be mounted face upwards in such a

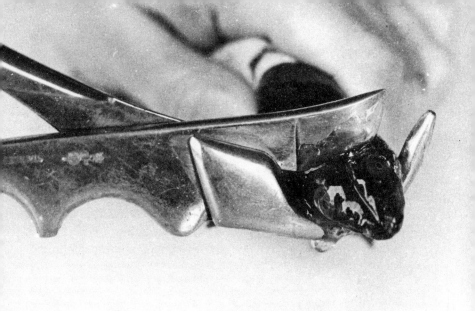

Illus 25 Rib-forceps, used to open the skull of an eel for extraction of the otoliths

medium as 'Isopon', a fibreglass resin which sets hard but is sufficiently viscous when soft to hold the specimen upright. The treated specimen must be immersed in an optically dense medium for examination. The transparent resins sold in toy moulding kits are ideal.

Population studies are the basis of all sound planning for conservation. In the case of hunted food animals, such as eels, conservation must be undertaken not so much for the preservation of an interesting animal but more for the well-being of the thousands of fishermen who depend upon it. Eel fishing and eel processing are highly specialised and very localised pursuits. Therefore a man who depends on eels may find it very difficult or quite impossible to change to another fish if the eel stocks disappear.

The slow growth and fantastic migrations of the freshwater eel make its study difficult but not impossible. At present, opinions on eel stocks vary so widely that doom-watchers can easily find evidence that the eel will become extinct and optimists can produce counter-statements with equal facility. The continued study of eels leads in two directions. Understanding the habits improves the efficiency of hunting but adds to the threat to the continued existence of the species. The accumulation of facts about the population structure shows how fishing should be controlled to the lasting benefit of future generations of eel and fisherman alike.

9

THE ORDER OF EELS

The classification of any group of living creatures is a highly specialised discipline and one which gives rise to unending argument. Every time a new study of the anatomy of a group is undertaken, characteristics are discovered which lead to a revision of previous standards. In this book I follow the general arrangement given by Professor Peter Castle of Victoria University, Wellington, New Zealand, in the fifteenth edition of *Encyclopaedia Britannica*. This is the latest scheme available (published in 1974), drawn up by one of the foremost living authorities on the marine eels. Castle recognises four sub-orders and nineteen families.

The sub-orders are defined by differences in the structure of the skeleton. The significance of these variations is not at all clear and the system will probably be revised sooner or later when more information comes to hand. The families are more clearly defined. They have in turn been divided into about 140 genera and more than 500 species have been described.

This book makes no attempt to define the species. A descriptive list of eels would require a large volume and would be of value to very few workers since most biologists are concerned with the local fauna rather than a global one. National or regional handbooks on fishes deal adequately with the problems of recognition. This chapter therefore gives an outline of the families with comments on some of the better-known species or genera.

A comprehensive chapter on eels by Léon Bertin and A. Arambourg was published in 1958 in the French *Traité de*

Zoologie. A very useful little survey of the order is given by Castle in *Tuatara* (Victoria University College, New Zealand) and the west African species have been surveyed recently by J. Blache in the *Bulletin de l'Institut française d'Afrique Noire* for 1967 and 1968. Professor William Beebe described many species in the course of his deep-sea explorations and published his findings in *Zoologica*, the journal of the New York Zoological Society. Eels from the Philippines are covered in some detail by A. W. C. T. Herre in the Philippine Journal of Science for 1923; and one of the most detailed surveys is in Weber and de Beaufort's *The Fishes of the Indo-Australian archipelago*. Some interesting observations on the morays and garden eels are given by Cousteau in *Life and Death in a Coral Sea*. This list is far from comprehensive but studies on the marine eels are unfortunately very widely scattered in the scientific literature.

The common eel of Europe and north Africa is named *Anguilla anguilla* (Linnaeus). It is the species which Linnaeus in Sweden described under the name *Muraena anguilla* in 1758. In 1803 Shaw described it as *Anguilla vulgaris*, a name which was widely used until quite recently. The first *Anguilla* is the name of the genus, the second defines the species. *Anguilla* is the sole genus of the family Anguillidae or freshwater eels and this family is usually placed at the beginning of systems of classification of eels, being considered the most primitive or least specialised type.

There are about fourteen other species of freshwater eels, all belonging to the same genus *Anguilla*. Schmidt and later his associate Wilhelm Ege studied this genus in great detail. Their work was based both on museum material and on the collections made on a round the world exploration by the Danish vessel *Dana* from 1928 to 1930, sponsored by the Carlsberg Foundation. In spite of this intensive work the exact number of species is not certain.

The *Anguilla* eels are divided into three groups on the basis of two external features: the skin colour may be marbled or uniform – in each case shading to a paler tone on the underside.

The marbled species all live in tropical or sub-tropical rivers which enter the Indian or Pacific Oceans. Eels with uniform colouring can have long or short dorsal fins. In the long-finned forms, which include the two Atlantic species, the origin of the dorsal fin lies well forward of the anal. In the short-finned, the dorsal begins almost opposite to the anal or a little way behind it. In some regions, such as New Zealand and south-western Australia, these characteristics (Illus 4) are sufficient to distinguish the species which occur there.

Two more sets of characters are needed to distinguish the species of the world. The first is the pattern of teeth on the vomer and the second is the number of vertebrae. The European eel has from 110 to 119 while the American *A. rostrata* has 103 to 111. These vertical counts overlap at the extremes, but the great majority of European eels have 113 to 117 and the Americans 105 to 109 so that even in quite a small sample there is every chance of finding some specimens which can be recognised with certainty.

The vertebral counts of the European eels, together with the ratios of such body measurements as total length to snout-to-anus length, are so constant that they support beyond any reasonable doubt the theory that the Sargasso is the sole breeding place. If, for instance, the eels of rivers flowing into the Mediterranean spawned there, it is more than likely that they would have developed characteristics distinct from those of an oceanic race.

All fifteen species of *Anguilla* have the same life cycle of an ocean birth place and a long larval migration while the major period of growth is spent in fresh water or in coastal sea water or lagoons. At a certain stage of growth they change their appearance and begin a migratory journey to the ocean. The skin turns silvery and any marbled pattern disappears. The eyes enlarge and feeding ceases. This approach towards sexual maturity is associated with the deposition of great reserves of fatty material in the muscle tissues and elsewhere. The fat is a reserve of food which the eel will now consume : part of it going to the developing eggs or sperm and part to supply the energy needed for the migration to the spawning grounds.

The broad similarity between the various species of *Anguilla*, both in appearance and habits, allow two inferences to be drawn. Firstly the structure of the freshwater eel is a highly successful development in evolution, the form is so perfect that no further adaptations were needed to allow the eels to thrive in an astonishing variety of climates and habitats. Secondly, the genus clearly originated in deep, warm water of the Indo-Pacific regions and spread from there to other parts of the world. While the adults can thrive in cold water, depth and high temperature remain essential requirements for breeding.

The Heterenchelyidae are burrowing eels in which the reduction of the fins has been carried to its conclusion, pectorals are absent and even the median fins are scarcely visible. The trunk is much shorter than the long tail. The teeth are small and the mouth large, suitable for a diet of invertebrates. They are known only from the tropical coasts of the Atlantic.

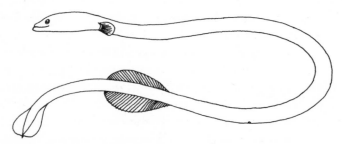

Illus 26   Moringua bicolor, worm eel

Small worm eels, Moringuidae, look remarkably like earthworms. The eyes are minute and the head is very long. The body is long but the tail is relatively short, pectoral fins are small and the median fins are confined to the tail. In some species the fins decrease in height before the tail tip is reached, giving the body the appearance of a feathered arrow. With a length of 1m one of the biggest is *Moringua javanica*, whose range extends from Indonesia to Japan. Other species are much smaller. The family is tropical, known from the Indo-Pacific and western Atlantic. The usual habitat is mud, sand or gravel in shallow water where the worm eels bury themselves. Several species enter brackish water. *M. bicolor* (Illus 26) has been described as 'pelagic' (swimming in the surface waters), while other species are recorded from burrows in the mud. Possibly, like the Atlantic sand eels, Ammodytidae, some worm eels alternate between the two habitats : feeding in the surface waters and digging in to the sea bed for rest or shelter. *M. javanica* lives close to the shore and prefers brackish water at the mouths of rivers.

The Xenocongridae or false morays are similar to the true morays but distinguished from them by details of the skull structure. They are burrowing eels found near the coasts of all tropical oceans.

The Muraenidae are the moray eels, well-known for their frequent large size, bright colours and predatory habits. They have neither scales nor pectorals and in some even the median fins are greatly reduced. The mouth is large, its opening extending well behind the eye and, except in the zebra morays, the teeth are strong and sharp in one or more rows on the jaws and palate. There is also a double row of strong, hooked teeth further back in the gullet, on the pharyngeal bones. The gill openings are very small. The morays nearly all live in shallow coastal water, especially amongst coral reefs and, in common with so many of the coral fishes, have developed bright colours with contrasting patterns. *Muraena* fossils are known from the Miocene.

The typical morays belong to the genus *Muraena*. They have rather compressed bodies, sometimes exceedingly elongated and well-developed dorsal and anal fins. The tail is about equal in length to the forepart of the body. The best known is the Mediterranean moray.

Morays are essentially warm-water fish. *M. helena* (Illus 27), which measures up to 130cm, is the only species known on the

coasts of Europe. Plentiful in the Mediterranean and around
Spain and Portugal, it is very rare further north and unknown
beyond the English Channel. This is the only Mediterranean
species, but the numbers increase through the Red Sea and into
the Indian and western Pacific oceans. Eighteen species are
known from Sri Lanka and twice as many from the East Indies.
About thirty are found on the American Pacific coast.

Muraena schismatorhynchus of Java and Sumatra has an
exceptionally long and slender snout with a pair of trumpet-
shaped nostrils at the tip. The freshwater moray *Gymnothorax
polyuranodon*, found from India and Sri Lanka through Indonesia to Fiji, lives in rivers and estuaries. Another widely distributed species, the white-spotted moray, *G. punctatus* sometimes
enters fresh water and is considered to have poisonous flesh.

Illus 27   Muraena Helena, moray eel

The giant moray, *Thyrsoidea macrura*, is probably the
biggest of all known eels, a truly magnificent fish reaching a
length of over 3m. The body is slender and slightly compressed
and the colour is a uniform greyish brown on the under parts.
It lives in shallow water and lagoons over a wide range, from
Natal through India and Sri Lanka to Formosa and Queensland.
It sometimes enters fresh water.

Perhaps the most remarkable members of the family are

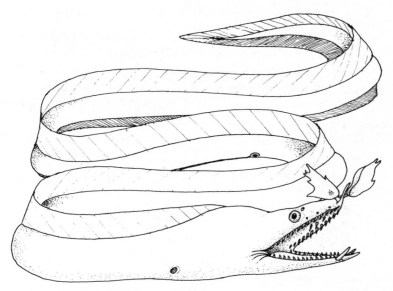

Illus 28 Rhinomuraena, leaf-nosed eel

the two species of leaf-nosed morays, *Rhinomuraena* (Illus 28). *R. quaesita* is found on the Marshall Islands and *R. ambonensis* only on the Ambon and Banda Islands of Indonesia. *R. ambonensis* reaches a length of 1m with a slender, rather compressed body and a very compressed head. It is coloured bright blue in front, shading to lavender on the tail while the anal fin is black with a white margin. There are three barbels on the lower lip and one on the tip of the snout. But the really striking feature is the form of the first pair of nostrils. These are short tubes which flare out into leaf-shaped attachments, an extreme development of the organs of sense and touch which are found in so many eels.

The reduction of the fins in the family is most pronounced in the genus *Gymnomuraena* of the Indian and western Pacific oceans. Dorsal and anal fins are both confined to the tip of the tail where they merge with the caudal to form a continuous fringe. These eels are less than 1m in length and live amongst reefs or near the shore.

The zebra moray, *Arndha zebra*, found from the Red Sea to Malagasy and the Philippines, is a most impressive fish : brown or black in colour with zebra-like stripes of white or pale yellow encircling the body. It reaches more than 1m in length. The closely related *Echidna* lives in rock crevices and is plentiful on the west African coast. These morays differ from the others in having some blunt and molar-like teeth and in feeding on small crustaceans. The adults are especially fond of crabs.

The Myrocongridae are ribbon-shaped eels found in the south Atlantic. They have pectoral fins but no scales, although there are said to be traces of pockets for scales in the skin. The teeth are rasp-like. Very little is known about the family.

The snipe eels, family Nemichthyidae, are relatively well-known. Many specimens were collected by the *Dana*, and later, William Beebe, courageous deep-sea explorer and erudite zoologist, studied them in the course of the New York Zoological Society's Bermuda Oceanographic Expeditions. A detailed paper on their taxonomy was published in 1937. The snipe eels are characterised by immensely elongated bodies with as many as 500 vertebrae, compared with the more usual hundred or two. The snout is always more than half the length of the head and often several times as long as the distance from eye to pectoral fins. The resemblance to a snipe's beak is very clear in extreme cases. In the skull the supra-occipital is missing and several other bones such as the palatine and pterygoid may be completely absent.

The teeth are small, pointed and pointing backwards, forming a rasp-like pattern. Although the jaws seem thin and wiry they are strong, and the backward-sloping teeth offer quite a remarkable degree of resistance to anything trying to escape from them. Even a long-dead museum specimen will hold an investigator's finger firmly. One of the British Museum specimens contains a large shrimp, greater in diameter than the eel's body. Clearly the delicate-looking beak is an efficient instrument for gathering prey. The body cavity, incidentally, is tiny. In the longest and thinnest genus, *Nemichthys*, which may measure more than

1m, the head is one-twelfth of the length of the eel, while the thread-like tail is nearly a hundred times the length of the trunk. The fin membranes are greatly reduced or completely absent so that the fin rays make a spiny fringe along the body.

Nemichthys scolopaceus was collected off Bermuda from water between 1,000 and 2,000m down. However, small snipe eels were seen from Beebe's bathysphere in as little as 150m. This is a good example of the difficulty of collecting eels of any kind by netting methods which may be excellent for other fish. Records based solely on netted specimens would have suggested that these eels are confined to very deep water. Even so, there is little doubt that the snipe eels do prefer water of great depths. *N. scolopaceus* is very widely distributed in the Atlantic and has been recorded as far north as Sable Island Bank off Nova Scotia and the Iceland-Faroes ridge. It becomes more frequent further south and is sometimes found in the stomachs of larger fish. The species is cosmopolitan in warm seas.

There is one tantalising record of a snipe eel found clinging by its jaws to the tail of a large red snapper caught off Bermuda. Was it just taking a ride, or had it perhaps been searching for ectoparasites? The forceps-like beak might be perfect for finding these and detaching them.

Avocettina (Illus 29) is another cosmopolitan genus which is

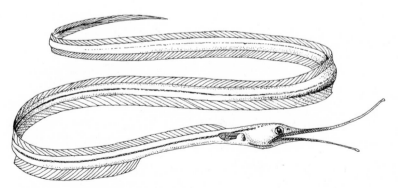

Illus 29 Avocettina, snipe eel

occasionally recorded in inshore waters, though normally living at great depths. The body is not so long as *Nemichthys* but is greatly compressed and ribbon-like. The jaws are so fine that they look more like needles but, as with *Nemichthys*, the fine, backward-pointing teeth offer great resistance to any movement against them, feeling as if they dig into the skin. The height of the fins is at least as great as the depth of the body and the eel gives the impression of being a long, disembodied fin. The presence of large pores on the lateral line gives *Avocettina* the name of porthole eel. The depth range is of the order of 1,000–9,000m and the majority of specimens have been recorded from the depths of the warmer parts of the oceans.

There have however been some extraordinary occurrences of *Avocettina*. *A. gilli* is known from a single specimen found off Alaska and described in 1890. One individual of the relatively common *A. infans* was found washed ashore in Cardigan Bay in Wales during a storm in 1927. Other genera include the Atlantic *Labichthys*, in which the vent lies almost directly underneath the base of the pectoral fin, giving the shortest body length of all. *Nematoprora* and *Cercomitus* are found in the Pacific but could well prove to be cosmopolitan.

Avocettinops (Illus 30), discovered at the bottom in deep water

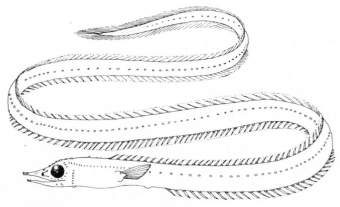

Illus 30   Avocettinops, soft-nosed eel

of the Caribbean, was placed in an order to itself at the time of its description in 1929 but has since been included in the Nemichthyidae. The head has a rather flabby feel because many of the bones are so reduced that they do not connect with each other. The eyes are enormous and the front nostrils are forward-pointing conical tubes. The teeth are small or completely absent, and presumably this odd eel hunts for invertebrates on the ocean bed.

The Serrivomeridae or saw-palates owe their name to the teeth on the palate of one genus, *Serrivomer*, which form a saw-like crest. They are rather small and thread-like eels with delicate-looking mouths. *Serrivomer beanii* has been very fully described by Beebe who found the species the commonest of the deep-sea eels in his study area off Bermuda. Fast swimmers with brilliantly iridescent bodies, they travel alone or in small groups, and feed on shrimps and krill. Larvae and adults of all sizes were found at all depths in the area, down to 500m. The longest adult recorded measured just under 60cm. *S. beanii* has been found as far north as the Grand Banks of Newfoundland and another species, *S. sector*, is found in the Indian and Pacific oceans, as far north as British Columbia.

Two other genera are known : *Platuronides* from the Atlantic and *Gavialiceps* in the Pacific. *Platuronides* has a false tail with a rhombic outline, formed by the elongation of dorsal and ventral rays just in front of the true tail tip. *Gavialiceps* is long and slender with a finely tapering tail. The snout is rather long and fine and the teeth very small.

The little species *Cyema atrum* which has a family, Cyemidae, to itself, lives at great depths in the oceans of the world. The body is shortened, with seventy-eight vertebrae at the most. The anal and dorsal fins are separated by a rudimentary tail. The fin rays of dorsal and anal fins lengthen towards the tail so that, while the body tapers to a fine point, the fins increase in height and the outline of the eel is almost parallel-sided with a slightly forked tail. The snout is a long beak, like that of the snipe eels.

171

The leptocephalus of *Cyema* has a very much deeper body than those of other eels, so that it looks like a beech leaf where the others resemble willows. Whatever may be the function of these extraordinary developments, the world-wide distribution of *Cyema* is a clear indication of perfect adaptation to uncommonly difficult surroundings.

The conger eels, family Congridae, are found around the world from shallow seas to the depths of the oceans. A few species extend their ranges into fresh water. Pectoral fins are present, but no scales, and the median fins extend in an unbroken line around the tail. Superficially congers resemble freshwater eels, but the mouth is always large and the lower jaw is shorter than the upper so that the opening lies just below the snout rather than at the tip. The teeth are large and strong, in accordance with their fierce predatory habits. Several genera are known from Eocene fossils.

One species, *Conger conger*, inhabits European waters. On the western Atlantic coast it is replaced by the very similar *Conger oceanicus* of North America and the same species, or a closely related one, lives on the coast of South America. *Conger oceanicus* is seldom found north of Cape Cod and only the leptocephali have been recorded in Canadian waters. On both sides of the Atlantic therefore the freshwater eel's range extends well to the north of the conger's. The depth range in the Atlantic reaches down to 250m. They usually retire from the coast into deeper waters for the winter, at least in the northern parts of their range.

Conger conger populations are found in the Indian and western Pacific oceans but, like the freshwater eels, no members of the genus have reached the American Pacific coasts. A similar species, the Indian conger *Conger cinereus*, is widely distributed in the Indo-Pacific, from the Red Sea and east African coasts to Japan and the Sandwich Islands. It is an important commercial fish.

Although congers and freshwater eels are considered to be distinctly separated on anatomical grounds, their distribution and ecology give some ground for believing that they are in fact closely related. The existence of very similar eastern and western Atlantic species, absence from the eastern Pacific and apparent incompatibility of habitats could all derive from a fairly late divergence from a single ancestral form.

The lesser conger, *Arisoma anago* (*Congrellus anago*), is a relatively small species with pointed teeth, not united to form a cutting edge. The eyes are large and the jaws small. It lives in shallow water close to the shore from the coast of Coromandel to Malaysia and Japan. Other members of the genus are found from the southern Atlantic through the Mediterranean to Hawaii and Fiji, both in shallow water and at considerable depths. *Arisoma bowersi* shares the need of many congers for great depths at spawning time : females kept in aquaria become egg-bound, their bodies swell to three times the normal size and they eventually burst.

The slender congers, *Uroconger*, have elongated bodies with long whip-like tails. The teeth are numerous and sharp, sloping backwards with several large canine on the upper lips. *Uroconger* has a very wide distribution with a wide range of habitats. *U. lepturus* lives in shallow, coastal water from India to the Philippines while *U. braueri* inhabits water down to 1,000m from east Africa to Sumatra. *U. varidens* has succeeded in crossing the Pacific and is known from Peruvian waters. *Promyllantor purpureus* reaches a depth of more than a mile (1,660m) in the Arabian Sea. The garden eels, *Heteroconger*

Illus 31 Heteroconger, garden eel

(Illus 31), have remarkable burrowing and feeding habits (page 44).

The conger pikes, *Muraenesocidae* (Illus 32), are formidable looking eels, large with powerful jaws armed with strong canine teeth, in a ridge on the vomer or palate as well as on the jaws. They are found in tropical water of all oceans, mainly on the coasts. Blache gives a description of *Cynoponticus ferox* which grows to 1½m and is abundant on sandy or muddy bottoms off the west African coast from 10–100m; from 70m downwards only very large specimens are found. They eat anything : large and small fish, crustaceans and even molluscs. *Muraenesox cinereus*, widely distributed in the Indian and Pacific oceans, is a fine eel, measuring up to 2m. It lives in brackish and sometimes even fresh water. The flesh is very good to eat and the conger pikes are caught in large quantities.

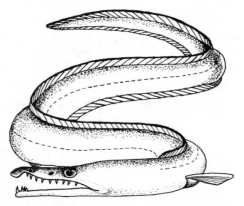

Illus 32   Muraenesox, conger pike

Hoplunnis has a very long body and differs from typical conger pikes in having small, conical teeth. It can be caught in the shallows at night and off the west African coast may move to deep water in the daytime.

The sorcerers, family Nettastomatidae, are a small group of deep-sea eels, with long, thin tapering bodies and beak-like jaws. They are found in warm water from 90–2,000m down, the range extending as far north as North Carolina and Japan. The tail section is reduced to a narrow filament but the median fins continue as a fringe around it. The eyes are large and the mouth-opening extends behind them. In front of the eyes the head is a long, narrow cone, and in *Venefica* the snout is prolonged into a fleshy flap. One pair of nostrils are long slits, situated close to the eye while the others are tubular and lie just behind the fleshy part of the snout. There are rows of large pores opening into sensory canals on the head and on the lateral line. The overall picture is of a fish with exceptionally well-developed organs of touch and smell, valuable for an inhabitant of deep, dark water. *Nettastoma* is known from Eocene fossils to the present.

The duck-billed eels, Nessorhamphidae, are Atlantic deep-sea eels. They breed in the Sargasso or close to it and make long migrations as they feed and grow. *Nessorhamphus ingolfianus* has been recorded as far north as Canada. The food is schizopods and shrimps, which are swallowed head first.

The Derichthyidae are distinguished from the conger family by their upper jaws which have a peculiar structure and are armed with rather small teeth (see Beebe, 1935). The premaxillary which, in most eels, is part of a single composite bone, is almost free and rather wide, forming an unusually wide upper lip and giving the eels their rather blunt-snouted appearance. They are found in the open water in deep seas, mainly between 220 and 1,000m down. In Beebe's explorations off Bermuda they were found singly and had been feeding on shrimps.

The snake eels, Ophichthidae, may be completely finless or may have well-developed dorsal and anal fins present except at the tip of the tail. Other members of the family have a full complement of fins including the pectorals. They are generally long, round-bodied eels with large gill chambers making the heads unusually prominent. The branchiostegal rays, which support the gill chamber, may number as many as twenty-five in contrast with the six or seven or so found in most fishes and the majority of eels. Fossil Ophichthids are known from the Eocene and Miocene.

The colours of the snake eels are often bright with contrasting patterns since they are essentially fish of shallow water, especially coral reefs. They burrow in mud or sand or in crevices in reefs, entering their refuges tail-first. A number of species have crossed the Pacific and are known from the American coasts, and the family is well represented in the Atlantic from Florida to Brazil.

Snake eels have not been recorded from the north-western coasts of Europe but a number are found in the Mediterranean. Amongst them is the magnificent serpent eel, *Ophichthys serpens*, which reaches a length of 2m. A single species, *Omochelys cruentifer*, has once been recorded from Canadian waters – from the stomach of a swordfish. It is found more frequently towards the south. *Omochelys* is a small eel with a long, narrow body and blunt snout, and the suggestion has been made that it is a lamprey-like parasitic boring fish. The longest on record measured 40cm and the depth range runs to over 400m.

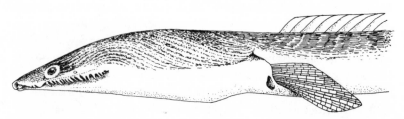

Illus 33 Cirrhimuraena, barbelled eel

The *Cirrhimuraena* (Illus 33) are rather small, usually less than 50cm. The pectoral fins are well-developed and the head is long with a very long mouth, the gape extending far behind the eye. The upper lips bear a series of barbels which form a fringe all the way along the jaws. The eyes are small, the front nostrils tubular while the hind pair are slits on the inner sides of the upper lip. This apparatus is presumably developed for smelling

176

and feeling for invertebrates on the bottom of the shallow water where these eels live.

Less pronounced equipment for hunting bottom-dwelling invertebrates is found in *Leiuranus* of the western Pacific and *Callechelys* which is found on both sides of that ocean and as far west as the Red Sea. They both have snouts which extend in front of the lower lip so that the opening of the mouth is on the lower side and the front nostrils point downwards. *Sphagebranchus* too has an underslung mouth and even the gill openings have moved towards the underside and may lie completely beneath the head.

Pisoodonophis (often placed in the genus of *Ophichthys*) has a very long, nearly cylindrical body with pectoral and median fins well developed. At least one species, *P. hypselopterus*, of Borneo, swims up rivers and several live in estuaries.

Also included in the family are the little worm eels, *Echelys,* whose median fins form a continuous fringe around the tail. They are mostly between 10 and 20cm in length, living in warm, shallow, sandy waters and on coral reefs.

The Macrocephenchelyidae are rare and little-known deep-sea eels from the Pacific.

The cut-throat eels, family Synaphobranchidae, are very common in deep water from 600–4,000m, but frequently move into shallower regions. Probably the most familiar of deep-sea eels, they take bait regularly and are quite often caught in trawl nets. The teeth are small and sharp and a diet of fish seems likely. The bodies are typically eel-like with a rather large mouth, opening at the tip of the snout. The name of the family refers to the extraordinary gill openings, unique among eels and rather rare in other fishes. The openings lie on the lower side of the throat where they form a single, V-shaped aperture, although the gills on each side are separated from each other within. There are two genera : *Histiobranchus* with a normal dorsal fin and *Synaphobranchus* which has a further peculiarity; the dorsal fin is reduced to a low, fringing structure and begins well behind the anal.

177

Cray's cut-throat eel, *Synaphobranchus kaupi* (*S. pinnatus*), is very widely distributed in the Atlantic where it has been reported south of Iceland down to Brazil. It, or a closely related form, is known from the Arabian Sea and the Pacific. Eggs and spawn of this species have been found, and Bigelow and Schroder tell of the capture of many males and females to the east of Cape Cod at about 900m down. This happened in June 1949; the biggest specimens were just over 60cm in length and one female had spawned, while others had well-developed gonads. Apparently survival after spawning is a possibility in this species.

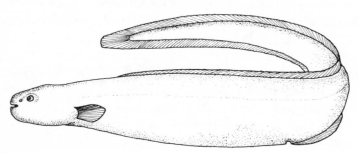

Illus 34   Simenchelys, slime eel

The slime eels, family Simenchelyidae, are snub-nosed, fat and very slimy. One of the two genera, *Simenchelys* (Illus 34), possesses scales but the other, *Gymnosimenchelys*, has none. The mouth is small and opens at the tip of the snout, on each jaw there is a single row of teeth and the tongue is large and strong.

One species, *S. parasiticus*, is known from the north Atlantic continental slopes and a similar, perhaps identical, one lives in Japanese waters. They are familiar to deep-sea fishermen who find them attached to the host species, but they can also lead an independent life at the bottom.

The final family is the Dysommidae, deep-sea eels of all the oceans with exceptionally wide-opening mouths. The suspensor bones, which support the hinge of the jaw, are directed backwards instead of downwards or forwards, an arrangement which allows for the wide gapes. Like other abyssal fishes these eels live in regions where prey is thinly distributed, and a predator which can take in a large morsel has an advantage over those which must hunt for smaller organisms.

Of the nineteen families outlined, all the members of one normally enter fresh water. Seven are found mainly in shallow water and may include frsehwater species while the remaining eleven are deep-sea eels. However, the eleven families of deep-water eels are small ones with few known species. No doubt more will be discovered in time but the depths of the oceans are uniformly dark and cool. While the animals that live there must be highly specialised to survive, they are not required to adapt themselves to the great variety of habitats found in the shallows. Therefore the actual number of species is likely to be relatively small.

While the shallow-water eels, represented by only seven families, show less pronounced variations in form, they contain the great majority of the species. Differences in depths, salinities and the nature of the sea bed all call for the small distinctions in form and colour which define separate species. The snake eels and the morays in particular have fulfilled this need with their marvellous variety of shapes, sizes, colours and feeding habits.

APPENDIX

Tables 1–3 give a summary of measurements, age distributions and foo
preferences of eels caught by fyke nets during my studies. Table 4 is a comple
list of seventy-eight species of food animals eaten by the eels of lakes on th
river Shannon and its tributaries. The tables are based on a series of papers o
the eels published in *Irish Fisheries Investigations*.

Table 1 : Length distributions (in centimetres to nearest
whole number downwards as a percentage of *n*, where
n = number of eels in sample)

	25–34	35–39	40–44	45–49	50–59	60–69	70–79	*n*	*Mean*	*Stan erro*
SHANNON LAKES										
Derg	1	11	27	27	29	4	1	271	47.4	0.76
Key	1	6	18	21	31	18	5	365	52.5	0.70
FERGUS LAKES										
Gash	4	19	21	28	21	4	1	71	46.2	1.04
Fin	0	30	40	20	10	0	0	49	43.2	0.65
CORRIB LAKES										
Corrib	14	30	21	18	11	4	2	349	41.3	0.87
Mask	6	19	34	22	11	7	0	77	44.1	1.22
Carra	1	14	28	20	30	5	0	71	47.6	0.95
ERNE LAKES										
Upper Erne	4	14	21	17	24	17	3	272	49.5	0.64
Dromore	1	2	19	25	40	12	1	220	50.7	0.50
OTHER LAKES										
Conn	17	46	21	8	8	0	0	84	39.6	0.65
Arrow	3	16	22	17	28	9	5	177	49.2	0.76
Gill	16	45	21	7	6	4	1	124	40.6	0.69
RIVERS										
Barrow	1	11	25	22	37	4	0	206	47.7	0.48
Blackwater	17	10	11	10	27	19	6	99	49.9	1.30
ESTUARIES										
Broadmeadow	12	30	23	20	13	1	1	168	42.4	0.59
S. Sloblands	6	25	31	23	10	4	1	408	44.1	0.42
Blackwater	25	17	23	14	14	6	1	1809	42.5	0.29
Shannon	6	13	13	14	25	22	7	244	51.4	0.94

Table 2: Age distributions (years of freshwater life as a percentage of n, where n=number of eels in sample)

	5–6	7–8	9–10	11–12	13–14	15–16	17–18	19–20	21–26	n
SHANNON LAKES										
Derg	1	8	22	32	22	10	4		1	259
Key		3	12	30	26	17	9	2	1	256
FERGUS LAKES										
Gash	17	43	26	11		2	2			66
Fin		12	47	30	10					50
CORRIB LAKES										
Corrib	2	13	32	25	16	8	3			331
Mask		7	31	28	17	8	5	1	3	75
Carra		7	27	32	25	7	1	1		68
ERNE LAKES										
Upper Erne	6	36	37	18	3					233
Dromore	2	18	45	30	4	1				205
OTHER LAKES										
Conn		19	37	27	14	3				
Arrow			25	38	20	7	4	1	5	85
Gill		6	38	35	13	6	2			95
RIVERS										
Barrow		1	14	36	34	19	2	1		107
Blackwater		2	19	18	22	13	9	4	13	171
ESTUARIES										
Broadmeadow	10	49	33	8						168
S. Sloblands	10	30	22	20	9	5	2	1	1	91
Blackwater	13*	43	22	10	5	4	3			102
Shannon		24	24	19	19	5	6	3		21

* (includes two 4 year specimens)

Appendix

Table 3: Frequency of occurrence of principal food items in eel stomachs (percentage of n, where n=number of stomachs containing food)

	Length of eel (cm)	*Asellus*	*Gammarus*	Ephemeroptera	Trichoptera	Chironomidae	Gastropoda	Fish	n
SHANNON LAKES									
Derg	all	82		12	44	32	49	4	105
Key	all	47	4	43	10	20	33	2	140
FERGUS LAKES									
Gash	all	35	6		6	47	47	41	17
Fin	all	42	17	22	6	58	64		36
CORRIB LAKES									
Corrib	30–49	32	38	11	24	42	27	12	128
	50–90	10	13		7	13	10	69	29
Mask	30–49	76	24	42	18	28	52	4	50
	50–80					7	14	71	14
Carra	all	10	37	31	10	26	47	16	19
ERNE LAKES									
Upper Erne	all	17	5	10	30	80		14	81
Dromore	all	11			39	33	11	56	18
OTHER LAKES									
Conn	all	22	32	27	40	30	56	5	63
Arrow	30–49	79	17	30	4	17	13		47
	50–79	89	38	38	27	27	47	11	45
Gill	30–49	22	37	46	58	14	20	10	59
	50–72		14		14			71	7
RIVERS									
Barrow	all	92			15	15		1	78
Blackwater	30–39	17	26	73	17	52	4	17	23
	40–49	12	23	6	6	6		64	17
	50–59	3		3	3			80	31

	Length of eel (cm)	Polychaeta	Mysidacea	*Gammarus*	Decapoda	Chironomidae	Gastropoda	Fish	n
ESTUARIES									
Broadmeadow	30–49	71			18		11	14	28
	50–75	40			90			10	10
S. Sloblands	30–49		43	19		100	25		16
	50–90					60		80	5
Blackwater	30–49		18	62		2	12	15	78
	50–85							100	3
Shannon	all		17	8	64			33	12

Appendix

Table 4: List of food organisms found in eels from seven lakes on the river Shannon, Ireland. Those marked with an asterisk were present in more than 10 per cent of all stomachs.

Oligochaete worms
Leeches:
  Piscicola geometra
  Glossiphonia heteroclita
  Helobdella sp.
Crustaceans:
  Cladocera
  *Asellus aquaticus
  A. meridianus
  Gammarus lacustris
  G. duebeni
  Mysis relicta
Anisoptera larvae
Zygoptera larvae
Hemiptera:
  Aphelocheirus montandoni
  Callicorixa praeusta
  Corixa semistriata
  Sigara distincta
  S. dorsalis
  Arctocoriza germari
Ephemeroptera larvae
  *Ephemera danica
  Ephemerella ignita
  Caenis horaria
  C. moesta
  Baetis pumilus
  Heptagenia sp.
Sisyra larva
Nymphula larva
Beetle larvae:
  Dytiscidae
  Gyrinidae
  Haliplidae
  Chrysomelidae
Caddis larvae:
  Polycentropus kingi
  P. flavomaculatus
  Holocentropus picicornis
  H. dubius
  Cyrnus flavidus
  C. trimaculatus
  Ecnomus sp.
  Hydropsyche sp.

Tinodes waeneri
Phryganea sp.
Limnephilus decipiens
L. flavicornis
L. lunatus
L. vittatus
Anabolia nervosa
Athripsodes aterrimus
A. cinerea
A. fulvus
A. senilis
Mystacides azurea
M. longicornis
Ocetis ochracea
Molanna angustata
Lepidostomum hirtum
Dipteran larvae:
  *Chironomidae (and pupae)
  Chaoborus
  Simulium
  Dicranota
  Limnophora
  Muscidae
  Tabanidae
Molluscs:
  Theodoxus fluviatilis
  Bithynia tentaculata
  Valvata piscinalis
  Potamopyrgus jenkinsi
  Physa fontinalis
  Lymnaea stagnalis
  *L. peregra
  Planorbis carinatus
  P. alba
  P. contortus
  Anodonta
  Sphaerium
  Pisidium
Fish:
  Eel
  Pike
  Perch
  Stickleback
TOTAL 78

REFERENCES

In recent years research work on eels in Europe has been co-ordinated largely by EIFAC, the European Inland Fisheries Advisory Commission, a section of the Food and Agriculture Organisation of the United Nations. Another important body in eel research is the International Council for the Exploration of the Sea which has a long established connection with the classical studies on migration. Both of these organisations now collaborate in eel work and held a joint conference on eel research in Helsinki in 1976.

Beebe, W. 'Deep Sea Fishes of the Bermuda Oceanographic Expeditions', *Zoologica*, 20 (1935) – 22 (1937)

Bertin, L. *Eels, a Biological Study* (1956)

Bertin, L. and Arambourg, C. 'Ordre des Anguilliformes', *Traité de Zoologie* (1958), 2,314–26

Bigelow, H. B. and Schroder, W. C. 'Fishes of the Gulf of Maine', *US Fish and Wildlife Service, Bulletin 74* (1953), 150–60

Blache, J. 'Contributions à la Connaissance des Poissons Anguilliformes de la Côté Occidentale d'Afrique', *Bulletin de l'Institut Française d'Afrique Noire*, 29A (1967); 30A (1968)

Boëtius, I. and J. 'Studies on the European Eel, *Anguilla anguilla* (L)', *Meddelser fra Danmarks Fiskeri- og Havundersogelser*, 4 (1967), 339–405

Brandt, A. von. *Fish Catching Methods of the World* (1964)

Burnet, A. M. R. 'Studies on the Ecology of the New Zealand Long-finned Eel, *Anguilla dieffenbachii* Gray, *Australian Journal of Marine and Freshwater Research*, 3 (1955), 32–63

Cairns, D. 'Life-history of the Two Species of New Zealand Freshwater Eels', *New Zealand Journal of Science and Technology*, 23 (1941), 53–72

Castle, P. H. J. 'The World of Eels', *Tuatara*, 16 (1968), 85–97

184

References

Castle, P. H. J. 'Prospects for the New Zealand Freshwater Eel Industry', *Commercial Fishing*, 11 (1972), 10

——. 'Anguilliformes', *Encyclopaedia Britannica*, fifteenth edition (1974), 898–900

Castle, P. H. J. and Williamson, G. R. 'On the Validity of the Freshwater Eel Species *Anguilla ancestralis* Ege, from the Celebes', *Copeia*, 2 (1974), 569–70

Chepurnov, A. V., Ovchinnikov, V. V. and Mikhailenko, N. A. 'The Generation of Electrical Discharges by Young Eels *Anguilla anguilla* (L)', *Journal of Ichthyology*, 11 (1971), 137–9

Christensen, J. M. 'Burning of Otoliths, a Technique for Age Determination of Soles and Other Fish', *Journal de Conseil International pour l'Exploration du Mer*, 29 (1964), 73–81

Cousteau, J.-Y. *Life and Death in a Coral Sea* (1971)

Creutzberg, F. 'Discrimination between Ebb and Flood Tide in Migrating Elvers (*Anguilla vulgaris* Turt.) by means of Olfactory Perception', *Nature* 184 (1959), Supplement 25, pp 1961–62

Deelder, C. L. 'Synopsis of Biological Data on the Eel *Anguilla anguilla* (Linnaeus), 1758', *FAO Fisheries Synopsis* (1970)

——. 'A New Eel Trap Developed in the Netherlands', *EIFAC Technical Papers*, 14 (1971), 97–100

Dembinski, W. and Chmielewski, A. 'The Application of Electricity to the Fishing of Eels by Means of Trawls', *EIFAC Technical Papers*, 14 (1971), 159–62

Ege, V. 'A revision of the genus *Anguilla* Shaw', *Dana Rep*, 16 (1939), 256

Ehrenbaum, E. and Marukawa, H. 'Über Alterbestimmung und Wachstum Beim Aal', *Zeitschrift fur Fischerei und deren Hilfswissenschaften*, 14 (1913), 83–8

Fidora, M. 'Influenze die Fattori Ambientali Sull' Accrescimento e Sul Differenziamento Sessuale Delle Anguille', *Nova Thalassia*, 1 (1951), 9

Frost, W. E. 'Observations on the Food of Eels (*Anguilla anguilla*) from the Windermere Catchment Area', *Journal of Animal Ecology*, 15 (1946), 43–53

Gill, W. W. *Myths and Songs from the South Pacific* (1876), 77–81

Grigson, J. *Fish Cookery* (1973)

References

Halsband, E. 'Fishing for Eels by Means of Electricity', *EIFAC Technical Papers*, 14 (1971), 57–68

Havinga, B. 1943 (quoted by Deelder, 1970)

Herre, A. W. C. T. 'Philippine Eels', *Philippine Journal of Science*, 23 (1923), 123–236

Heuvelmans, B. *In the Wake of the Sea Serpents* (1968)

Hurley, D. A. 'The American Eel (*Anguilla rostrata*) in Eastern Lake Ontario', *Journal of the Fisheries Research Board of Canada*, 29 (1972), 535–43

Jubb, R. A. 'The Eels of South African Rivers and Observations on Their Ecology', in *Ecological Studies in Southern Africa*, ed D. H. S. Davis (1964)

Kaulin, K. 'Fishing for Eels with Longlines', *EIFAC Technical Papers*, 14 (1971), 31–8

Kennedy, M. *The Sea Angler's Fishes* (1969)

Klust, G. 'Eel Stownets in German Rivers', *EIFAC Technical Papers*, 14 (1971), 39–58

Kokhnenko, V. *The European Eel*, translated by Fisheries Research Board of Canada (Moscow, 1969)

Lowe, R. H. 'The Influence of Light and Other Factors on the Seaward Migration of the Silver Eel (*Anguilla anguilla* L.)', *Journal of Animal Ecology*, 21 (1952), 275–309

Mann, H. 'Beobachtungen uber den Aalaufstieg in der Aalleiter an der Staustufe Geesthacht in Jahra 1961', *Fischwirtschaft*, 13 (1963), 182–6

Matsui, I. 'Leptocephali of the Eel *Anguilla japonica* Found in the Water of Ryukyu Deep', *Journal of the Shimonoseki College of Fisheries*, 20 (1971), 13–18

Medcof, J. C. 'Incidental Records on Behaviour of Eels in Lake Ainslie, N.S.', *Journal of the Fisheries Research Board of Canada*, 23 (1966), 1,101–5

Meyer-Warden, P. F. and Aker, E. '*Aalbibliographie*', *Veröffentlichungen des Instituts für Küsten- und Binnenfischerei*, 39 (1966), 1–231

Mohr, H. 'The Effect of Some Behaviour Patterns on the Catching Techniques for Eel', *EIFAC Technical Papers*, 14 (1971), 27–30

Moriarty, C. 'Studies of the Eel *Anguilla anguilla* in Ireland' : 1–5, *Irish Fisheries Investigations* (1972–5)

References

Moriarty, C. 'A Technique for Examining Eel Otoliths', *Journal of Fish Biology*, 5 (1973), 183–4

Muus, B. J. 'The Fauna of Danish Estuaries and Lagoons', *Meddelser fra Danmarks Fiskeri- og Havundersogelser*, 5 (1967), 1–316

O'Leary, D. (1) 'A Low Head Elver Trap', (2) 'Experiments with Eel Nets in Ireland', *EIFAC Technical Papers*, 14 (1971), 129–42

Perrett, R. *Eels: How to Catch Them* (1958)

Rasmussen, C. J. 'Two Danish Finds of Female Eels (*Anguilla anguilla*) in Spawning or Partial Spawning Dress', Report Danish Biological Station (1951), 35–9

Rommel, S. A., jr, and McCleave, J. D. 'Oceanic Electric Fields : Perception by American Eels?' *Science*, 176 (1972), 1,233–5

Schaffer, E. Aale auf den Lande *Fisherbote* 11 (1919), 232–5

Schmidt, J. 'The Breeding Places of the Eel', *Philosophical Transactions Royal Society*, 211 (1922), 179–208

——. 'On the Distribution of the Fresh-water Eels (*Anguilla*) throughout the World. II, Indo-Pacific Region', *Mémoires de l'Académie des Sciences et des Lettres de Danemark*, 10 (1925)

Sinha, V. R. P. and Jones, J. W. *The European Freshwater Eel* (1975)

Skrsynski, W. 'Review of Biological Knowledge of New Zealand Freshwater Eels (*Anguilla* spp.)', *Fisheries Technical Report New Zealand Ministry of Agriculture and Fisheries*, 109 (1974), 1–37

Smith, M. W. and Saunders, J. W. 'The American Eel in Certain Fresh Waters of the Maritime Provinces of Canada', *Journal of the Fisheries Research Board of Canada*, 12 (1955), 238–69

Smitt, F. A. *Scandinavian Fishes* (1895)

Stasko, A. B. and Rommel, S. A., jr. 'Swimming Depth of Adult American Eels (*Anguilla rostrata*) in a Saltwater Bay as Determined by Ultrasonic Tracking', *Journal of the Fisheries Research Board of Canada*, 31 (1974), 1,148–50

Steinberg, R. 'The method of two boats trawling for eels in freshwater', *EIFAC Technical Papers*, 14 (1971), 89–95

Svärdson, G. 'Eels (*Anguilla anguilla*) Found in Sweden in Partial Nuptial Dress', *Report of the Institute of Freshwater Research, Drottningholm*, 29 (1949), 129–34

References

Svärdson, G. 'The Predatory Impact of Eel (*Anguilla anguilla* L.) on Populations of Crayfish (*Astacus astacus* L.)', *Report of the Institute of Freshwater Research, Drottningholm*, 52 (1972), 149–191

Tesch, F. W. *Der Aal* (1973)
——. 'Speed and Direction of Silver and Yellow Eels, *Anguilla anguilla*, Released and Tracked in the Open North Sea', *Bericht der Deutschen Wissenschaftlichen Kommission fur Meeresforschung*, 23 (1974), 181–97
Thompson, W. *The Natural History of Ireland* (1856), 4, 222–30
Thurow, F. 'Dry substance and fat content of eel from the Kiel Bay and Kiel Fjord', *Arch Fischereiwiss*, 8, No. 1–2 (1957)
Trybom, F. and Schneider, G. 'Die Markierungsversuche mit Aalen und die Wanderungen Gekennzeichneter Aale in der Ostsee', *Rapports du Conseil International pour l'Exploration du Mer* 9 (1908), 51–9

Usui, A. *Eel Culture* (1974)

Vladykov, V. D. 'Remarks on the American Eel (*Anguilla rostrata* Le Sueur)', *Verhandlungen der Internationalen Vereinigung für Theoretische und Angewandte Limnologie*, 16 (1966), 1,007–17
——. 'Homing of the American Eel, *Anguilla rostrata,* as Evidenced by Returns of Transplanted Tagged Eels in New Brunswick', *Canadian Field Naturalist*, 85 (1971), 241–8

Weber, M. and de Beaufort, L. F. *The Fishes of the Indo-Australian Archipelago* (1911)
Went, A. E. J. 'Irish Fishing Spears', *Journal of the Royal Society of Antiquaries of Ireland*, 82 (1952), 109–34
Wheeler, A. 'Leonard Jenyns's Notes on Cambridgeshire Fishes', *Cambridge and Isle of Ely Naturalists' Trust Annual Report* (1973), 19–22

Yamamoto, K. and Yamamuchi, K. 'Sexual Maturation of Japanese Eel and Production of Eel Larvae in the Aquarium', *Nature*, 251 (1974), 220–22

ACKNOWLEDGEMENTS

My studies have been assisted by many people. I would like to mention in particular Miss Eileen Twomey and Professor J. N. R. Grainger. Dr Colm O'Riordan of the National Museum in Dublin and Mr Alwyne Wheeler of the British Museum (Natural History) very kindly helped me in examining eels in their collections. I gratefully acknowledge permission from Dr Michael Kennedy to quote from *The Sea Anglers' Fishes*, and from the Royal Society to quote from Johannes Schmidt's classical paper on *The Breeding Places of the Eel*.

Grateful thanks to Sally-Ann Shaw Smith who drew the diagrams and to Margaret Sinanan who typed skilfully from a hideous manuscript. Above all, thanks go to my wife who not only lived with the book in preparation but read it and made innumerable suggestions for its improvement.

All photographs are by the author

INDEX

Index

Index

Perca, 36, 98
perch, see Perca
pickled eels, 154
pike, see Esox
Pisidium (freshwater cockle), 183
Pisoodonophis, 177
plankton, 33
Platichthys (flounder), 37
Platuronides, 172
Pliny, 22
pollan, see Coregonus
pollution, 144
pond dimensions, 134
population density, 56
porthole eel, see Avocettina
pound net, 125
predation, 63
Promyllantor, 173
Putte, 29, 51

Redi, F., 22
Rhinomuraena, 167
rudd, see Erythrophthalmus

Salmo, (salmon and trout), 35
Salvelinus (char, brook trout), 35, 40
sampling methods, 156
sand eel, see Ammodytes
Saprolegnia, 147
Sargasso, 82
sardine, 137
scaly eel, see Brachiopterygian
scales, 47
sea lice, see Argulus
sea serpent, 26
seining, 116
seismic activity, 76
Serrivomer, 171
Serrivomeridae, 171
sex, 57
silver eel, 68
Simenchelyidae, 178
Simenchelys, 46, 178
Simulid, 40
skinning, 150
slime eel, see Simenchelys
smoked eel paté, 153
smoking, 150
snails, 34

snake eel, see Ophichthidae
snigling, 96
snipe eel, see Nemichthidae
sorcerer, see Veneficidae
spawning migration, 68
spear-fishing, 100
speed of swimming, 78
Sphagebranchus, 177
stickleback, see Gasterosteus
stomach contents, 30
storage, 143
stow net, 121
summer fyke, 54, 114
Synaphobranchidae, 177
Synaphobranchus, 177
Synbranchiformes, 18

tagging, 68, 72, 75
tail, 10
tanker lorry, 146
teleost, 18
temperature, 53, 60, 84, 130
thread-eel, see Nemichthidae
Thyrsoidae, 166
transportation, 146
traps, 101
trawling, 117
Trichoptera (caddis), 33, 183
tuna, 20, 127
trout, see Salmo

ultrasonic tracking, 68
Uroconger, 173

Venefica, 175

Walton, Izaak, 24, 96
Water fleas, see Cladocera
water lice, see Asellus
well boat, 147
whitefish, see Coregonus
white-spotted moray, see Gymnothorax
worm eel, see Moringuidae

Xenocongridae, 165

yellow eel, 66

zebra moray, see Arndha

192